50 Indian Brunch Recipes for Home

By: Kelly Johnson

Table of Contents

- Masala Omelette
- Poha (Flattened Rice)
- Aloo Paratha (Potato Stuffed Bread)
- Chole Bhature (Chickpea Curry with Fried Bread)
- Upma (Semolina Breakfast Porridge)
- Idli (Steamed Rice Cakes)
- Dosa (Fermented Rice Crepes)
- Uttapam (Savory Pancakes)
- Medu Vada (Lentil Fritters)
- Egg Curry
- Vegetable Cutlet
- Paneer Bhurji (Scrambled Cottage Cheese)
- Bread Pakora (Spiced Bread Fritters)
- Aloo Tikki (Potato Patties)
- Dhokla (Steamed Chickpea Flour Cake)
- Sabudana Khichdi (Tapioca Pearl Pilaf)
- Chana Masala (Spiced Chickpeas)
- Poori Bhaji (Fried Bread with Potato Curry)
- Masala Dosa
- Egg Bhurji (Scrambled Eggs)
- Rava Upma (Semolina Breakfast Porridge)
- Aloo Puri (Potato Stuffed Fried Bread)
- Moong Dal Cheela (Mung Bean Pancakes)
- Kachori (Stuffed Savory Pastry)
- Besan Cheela (Chickpea Flour Pancakes)
- Bread Upma (Bread Stir-fry)
- Matar Kulcha (Peas Curry with Flatbread)
- Egg Roll
- Methi Thepla (Fenugreek Flatbread)
- Vegetable Uttapam
- Anda Bhurji (Indian Style Scrambled Eggs)
- Sooji Dhokla (Semolina Steamed Cake)
- Misal Pav (Spicy Sprout Curry with Bread)
- Palak Paneer Paratha (Spinach Cottage Cheese Stuffed Bread)
- Ragi Dosa (Finger Millet Crepes)

- Akki Roti (Rice Flour Flatbread)
- Dal Pakwan (Lentil Curry with Fried Bread)
- Chana Chaat (Chickpea Salad)
- Bread Uttapam
- Egg Biryani
- Aloo Kachori (Potato Stuffed Savory Pastry)
- Rava Idli (Semolina Steamed Cakes)
- Sabudana Vada (Tapioca Pearl Fritters)
- Chutney Sandwich
- Chole Kulcha (Chickpea Curry with Flatbread)
- Egg Curry Puff
- Aloo Methi Paratha (Potato Fenugreek Stuffed Bread)
- Khaman Dhokla (Gram Flour Steamed Cake)
- Rajma Chawal (Kidney Bean Curry with Rice)
- Anda Pav (Egg Sandwich)

Masala Omelette

Ingredients:

- 2 eggs
- 1 small onion, finely chopped
- 1 small tomato, finely chopped
- 1 green chili, finely chopped (adjust according to spice preference)
- 2 tablespoons chopped coriander leaves
- 1/4 teaspoon turmeric powder
- 1/4 teaspoon red chili powder
- Salt to taste
- 1 tablespoon oil or ghee for cooking

Instructions:

1. In a mixing bowl, crack the eggs and beat them well until they are frothy.
2. Add chopped onions, tomatoes, green chili, coriander leaves, turmeric powder, red chili powder, and salt to the beaten eggs. Mix everything together until well combined.
3. Heat oil or ghee in a non-stick skillet over medium heat.
4. Pour the egg mixture into the skillet and spread it evenly to form a round omelette.
5. Let the omelette cook undisturbed for a minute or two until the bottom sets.
6. Using a spatula, gently lift the edges of the omelette to check if it has cooked and is lightly golden brown.
7. Once the bottom is cooked, carefully flip the omelette to cook the other side. Cook for another minute or until both sides are evenly cooked and golden brown.
8. Transfer the masala omelette to a plate and serve hot with bread, toast, or alongside your favorite chutney or ketchup.

Enjoy your delicious Masala Omelette!

Poha (Flattened Rice)

Ingredients:

- 1 cup thick or thin Poha (flattened rice)
- 1 medium-sized onion, finely chopped
- 1 medium-sized potato, peeled and diced into small cubes
- 1 small green chili, finely chopped (adjust according to spice preference)
- 1/4 cup peanuts
- 1/2 teaspoon mustard seeds
- 1/2 teaspoon cumin seeds
- 1 sprig of curry leaves
- 1/4 teaspoon turmeric powder
- Salt to taste
- 2 tablespoons oil
- Fresh coriander leaves for garnish (optional)
- Lemon wedges for serving (optional)

Instructions:

1. Rinse the poha in a colander under running water for a few seconds. Drain well and set aside.
2. Heat oil in a pan or skillet over medium heat.
3. Add mustard seeds and cumin seeds. Allow them to crackle.
4. Add peanuts and sauté until they turn golden brown.
5. Add chopped onions, diced potatoes, green chili, and curry leaves. Sauté until onions turn translucent and potatoes are cooked through, about 5-7 minutes.
6. Reduce the heat to low and add turmeric powder and salt. Mix well.
7. Add the rinsed poha to the pan and gently toss everything together until the poha is well coated with the spices and ingredients. Be gentle to avoid breaking the poha.
8. Cook for another 2-3 minutes, stirring occasionally, until the poha is heated through.
9. Turn off the heat and garnish with freshly chopped coriander leaves, if using.
10. Serve hot Poha with lemon wedges on the side for squeezing over the poha before eating.

Enjoy your flavorful Poha for breakfast or brunch!

Aloo Paratha (Potato Stuffed Bread)

Ingredients:

For the dough:

- 2 cups whole wheat flour (atta)
- Water, as needed
- Salt, to taste
- 1 tablespoon oil or ghee

For the potato filling:

- 3 medium-sized potatoes, boiled, peeled, and mashed
- 1 small onion, finely chopped
- 1 green chili, finely chopped (adjust according to spice preference)
- 1/2 teaspoon cumin seeds
- 1/2 teaspoon garam masala
- 1/2 teaspoon red chili powder (optional)
- 1/2 teaspoon amchur (dry mango powder) or chaat masala
- Salt, to taste
- Fresh coriander leaves, finely chopped (optional)
- Oil or ghee, for cooking

Instructions:

1. Prepare the dough:
    - In a mixing bowl, add the whole wheat flour and salt. Mix well.
    - Gradually add water and knead into a soft, smooth dough. Add oil or ghee and continue to knead for a few more minutes.
    - Cover the dough and let it rest for about 20-30 minutes.
2. Prepare the potato filling:
    - In a separate bowl, combine the mashed potatoes, chopped onion, green chili, cumin seeds, garam masala, red chili powder (if using), amchur or

chaat masala, salt, and coriander leaves (if using). Mix everything together until well combined.

3. Make the parathas:
   - Divide the dough into equal-sized balls, slightly larger than the potato filling balls.
   - Take one dough ball and flatten it slightly. Dust it with flour and roll it out into a small circle.
   - Place a portion of the potato filling in the center of the circle.
   - Gather the edges of the dough and seal the filling completely, ensuring there are no cracks.
   - Flatten the filled dough ball gently and dust it with flour.
   - Roll out the filled dough ball into a paratha, making sure it's neither too thick nor too thin.
   - Heat a tawa or skillet over medium-high heat. Once hot, place the rolled-out paratha on the tawa.
   - Cook for a minute or until small bubbles start to appear on the surface.
   - Flip the paratha and spread some oil or ghee on the cooked side.
   - Cook the other side until golden brown spots appear, pressing gently with a spatula.
   - Flip again and spread oil or ghee on this side as well. Cook until both sides are evenly cooked and golden brown.
   - Repeat the process with the remaining dough balls and potato filling.

4. Serve hot:
   - Remove the cooked parathas from the tawa and place them on a plate.
   - Serve hot Aloo Parathas with yogurt, pickle, chutney, or any side dish of your choice.

Enjoy your delicious Aloo Parathas!

Chole Bhature (Chickpea Curry with Fried Bread)

Ingredients:

For Chole (Chickpea Curry):

- 1 cup dried chickpeas (or 2 cans of cooked chickpeas)
- 2 tablespoons oil
- 1 large onion, finely chopped
- 2 tomatoes, finely chopped
- 2-3 green chilies, slit lengthwise
- 1 tablespoon ginger-garlic paste
- 1 teaspoon cumin seeds
- 1 teaspoon coriander powder
- 1 teaspoon cumin powder
- 1/2 teaspoon turmeric powder
- 1/2 teaspoon red chili powder (adjust to taste)
- 1 teaspoon garam masala
- Salt to taste
- 2 tablespoons chopped coriander leaves for garnish
- Water as needed

For Bhature (Fried Bread):

- 2 cups all-purpose flour (maida)
- 1/4 cup semolina (sooji)
- 1/4 cup plain yogurt (curd)
- 1/2 teaspoon baking powder
- 1/4 teaspoon baking soda
- Salt to taste
- 1 tablespoon sugar
- Water, as needed
- Oil for deep frying

Instructions:

For Chole (Chickpea Curry):

1. If using dried chickpeas, soak them in water overnight or for at least 6-8 hours. Then, pressure cook them with salt until soft. If using canned chickpeas, rinse them well under cold water.
2. Heat oil in a pan or pressure cooker. Add cumin seeds and let them splutter.
3. Add chopped onions and sauté until they turn golden brown.
4. Add ginger-garlic paste and slit green chilies. Sauté for a minute until the raw smell disappears.
5. Add chopped tomatoes and cook until they turn soft and mushy.
6. Add all the dry spices - coriander powder, cumin powder, turmeric powder, red chili powder, garam masala, and salt. Mix well and cook for a couple of minutes.
7. Add cooked chickpeas along with water (if using pressure cooker, adjust the consistency according to your preference). Bring the mixture to a boil, then simmer for about 10-15 minutes, allowing the flavors to meld together.
8. Garnish with chopped coriander leaves and keep the Chole warm until serving.

For Bhature (Fried Bread):

1. In a large mixing bowl, combine all-purpose flour, semolina, yogurt, baking powder, baking soda, salt, and sugar.
2. Gradually add water and knead the mixture into a soft, smooth dough. Cover the dough with a damp cloth and let it rest for at least 2 hours.
3. After resting, divide the dough into small balls. Roll each ball into a circle of about 6-7 inches in diameter.
4. Heat oil in a deep frying pan or kadai over medium-high heat.
5. Once the oil is hot, carefully slide in the rolled-out dough. Fry until it puffs up and turns golden brown on both sides. Press gently with a slotted spoon while frying to help it puff up evenly.
6. Remove the fried Bhature from the oil and drain excess oil on paper towels.

Serve hot Chole Bhature together, garnished with some chopped onions, lemon wedges, and pickle. Enjoy this delicious and indulgent dish!

Upma (Semolina Breakfast Porridge)

Ingredients:

- 1 cup semolina (rava/sooji)
- 2 tablespoons oil or ghee
- 1 teaspoon mustard seeds
- 1 teaspoon cumin seeds
- 1/2 inch ginger, finely chopped
- 1-2 green chilies, finely chopped (adjust according to spice preference)
- 1 medium-sized onion, finely chopped
- 1 small carrot, finely chopped (optional)
- 1 small capsicum (bell pepper), finely chopped (optional)
- 2 tablespoons green peas (fresh or frozen)
- 1/4 teaspoon turmeric powder
- Salt to taste
- 2 1/2 cups water
- Fresh coriander leaves for garnish (optional)
- Lemon wedges for serving (optional)

Instructions:

1. Dry roast the semolina:
    - Heat a dry skillet or pan over medium heat.
    - Add the semolina and roast it for about 5-6 minutes, stirring constantly, until it turns light golden brown in color and aromatic. Be careful not to burn it. Transfer the roasted semolina to a plate and set aside.
2. Prepare the Upma:
    - Heat oil or ghee in the same skillet or pan over medium heat.
    - Add mustard seeds and cumin seeds. Let them splutter.
    - Add chopped ginger and green chilies. Sauté for a minute.
    - Add chopped onions and sauté until they turn translucent.
    - If using, add chopped carrots, capsicum, and green peas. Cook for a few minutes until the vegetables are slightly softened.
    - Add turmeric powder and salt. Mix well.
    - Pour water into the skillet and bring it to a boil.

- Gradually add the roasted semolina to the boiling water, stirring continuously to prevent lumps from forming.
- Reduce the heat to low and cover the skillet. Let it simmer for 3-4 minutes, stirring occasionally, until the Upma thickens and the semolina is cooked through. If it becomes too thick, you can add a little more hot water.
- Once cooked, remove the skillet from heat.

3. Serve:
    - Garnish the Upma with freshly chopped coriander leaves, if using.
    - Serve hot Upma with a side of lemon wedges for squeezing over the Upma before eating.

Enjoy your warm and comforting Upma for breakfast or brunch!

Idli (Steamed Rice Cakes)

Ingredients:

For Idli Batter:

- 2 cups idli rice (parboiled rice)
- 1 cup whole or split urad dal (black gram lentils)
- 1 teaspoon fenugreek seeds (methi seeds)
- Water, as needed
- Salt to taste

For Steaming Idlis:

- Idli molds or plates
- Oil or ghee for greasing the molds

Instructions:

1. Prepare the Idli Batter:
    - Rinse the idli rice and urad dal separately under cold water until the water runs clear. Soak them in water separately for at least 4-6 hours, along with fenugreek seeds.
    - After soaking, drain the water from the rice and dal.
    - Grind the urad dal in a blender or wet grinder with enough water to make a smooth and fluffy batter. The consistency should be thick and airy. Transfer the batter to a large bowl.
    - Grind the soaked rice in the same blender or wet grinder, adding water gradually to make a smooth batter. The consistency should be slightly coarse compared to the urad dal batter.
    - Combine the rice batter with the urad dal batter in the large bowl. Mix well using your hands or a spoon until thoroughly combined.
    - Add salt to the batter and mix again. The batter should have a thick pouring consistency.

- Cover the bowl with a lid or cloth and let the batter ferment in a warm place for 8-12 hours or overnight. During fermentation, the batter will rise and double in volume.
2. Steam the Idlis:
    - Once the batter is fermented, mix it gently to deflate any air bubbles.
    - Grease the idli molds or plates with oil or ghee.
    - Pour a ladleful of batter into each mold, filling them about three-quarters full.
    - Prepare a steamer by adding water to the bottom pan and bringing it to a boil.
    - Place the idli molds or plates in the steamer and cover it with a lid.
    - Steam the idlis on medium-high heat for about 10-12 minutes, or until a toothpick inserted into the center comes out clean.
    - Once cooked, remove the idli molds from the steamer and let them cool for a few minutes.
    - Use a spoon or knife to gently remove the idlis from the molds.
3. Serve:
    - Serve the hot and fluffy idlis with sambar (lentil stew), coconut chutney, or any other accompaniment of your choice.

Enjoy your homemade Idlis as a wholesome and nutritious breakfast!

Dosa (Fermented Rice Crepes)

Ingredients:

For Dosa Batter:

- 2 cups raw rice (preferably parboiled rice)
- 1/2 cup urad dal (black gram lentils)
- 1/4 teaspoon fenugreek seeds (methi seeds)
- Water, as needed
- Salt to taste

For Making Dosas:

- Dosa tawa (griddle) or non-stick skillet
- Oil or ghee for greasing the tawa
- Spices (optional): cumin seeds, black mustard seeds, curry leaves

Instructions:

1. Prepare the Dosa Batter:
    - Rinse the rice and urad dal separately under cold water until the water runs clear. Soak them in water separately, along with fenugreek seeds, for at least 4-6 hours.
    - After soaking, drain the water from the rice and urad dal.
    - Grind the urad dal in a blender or wet grinder with enough water to make a smooth and fluffy batter. The consistency should be thick and airy. Transfer the batter to a large bowl.
    - Grind the soaked rice in the same blender or wet grinder, adding water gradually to make a smooth batter. The consistency should be slightly coarse compared to the urad dal batter.
    - Combine the rice batter with the urad dal batter in the large bowl. Mix well using your hands or a spoon until thoroughly combined.
    - Add salt to the batter and mix again. The batter should have a thick pouring consistency.

- Cover the bowl with a lid or cloth and let the batter ferment in a warm place for 8-12 hours or overnight. During fermentation, the batter will rise and double in volume.

2. Make Dosas:
    - Once the batter is fermented, mix it gently to deflate any air bubbles.
    - Heat a dosa tawa or non-stick skillet over medium-high heat.
    - Once the tawa is hot, sprinkle a few drops of water on it. If the water sizzles and evaporates immediately, the tawa is ready.
    - Grease the tawa lightly with oil or ghee using a small piece of cloth or onion.
    - Pour a ladleful of dosa batter onto the center of the tawa.
    - Using the back of the ladle, spread the batter in a circular motion to form a thin crepe. You can make it as thick or thin as you like.
    - Drizzle a little oil or ghee around the edges of the dosa and in the center.
    - Sprinkle any desired spices (optional) like cumin seeds, black mustard seeds, or curry leaves over the dosa.
    - Cook the dosa for 1-2 minutes on medium-high heat until the bottom turns golden brown and crisp.
    - Once the bottom is cooked, use a spatula to loosen the edges of the dosa and gently flip it over.
    - Cook the other side for another minute until it's lightly browned and crisp.
    - Remove the dosa from the tawa and serve hot.

3. Serve:
    - Serve dosas hot with sambar (lentil stew), coconut chutney, or any other accompaniment of your choice.

Enjoy your crispy and delicious dosas as a breakfast or snack!

Uttapam (Savory Pancakes)

Ingredients:

For Uttapam Batter:

- 1 cup parboiled rice
- 1/2 cup split urad dal (black gram lentils)
- 1/4 teaspoon fenugreek seeds (methi seeds)
- Water, as needed
- Salt to taste

For Toppings (Optional):

- Finely chopped onions
- Finely chopped tomatoes
- Finely chopped green chilies
- Finely chopped coriander leaves
- Grated carrots
- Sliced green bell peppers
- Other vegetables of your choice

For Making Uttapam:

- Uttapam tawa (griddle) or non-stick skillet
- Oil or ghee for cooking
- Spices (optional): cumin seeds, black mustard seeds, curry leaves

Instructions:

1. Prepare the Uttapam Batter:
    - Rinse the rice and urad dal separately under cold water until the water runs clear. Soak them in water separately, along with fenugreek seeds, for at least 4-6 hours.

- After soaking, drain the water from the rice and urad dal.
- Grind the urad dal in a blender or wet grinder with enough water to make a smooth and fluffy batter. The consistency should be thick and airy. Transfer the batter to a large bowl.
- Grind the soaked rice in the same blender or wet grinder, adding water gradually to make a smooth batter. The consistency should be slightly coarse compared to the urad dal batter.
- Combine the rice batter with the urad dal batter in the large bowl. Mix well using your hands or a spoon until thoroughly combined.
- Add salt to the batter and mix again. The batter should have a thick pouring consistency.
- Cover the bowl with a lid or cloth and let the batter ferment in a warm place for 8-12 hours or overnight. During fermentation, the batter will rise and double in volume.

2. Make Uttapam:
    - Once the batter is fermented, mix it gently to deflate any air bubbles.
    - Heat an Uttapam tawa or non-stick skillet over medium-high heat.
    - Once the tawa is hot, pour a ladleful of Uttapam batter onto the center of the tawa.
    - Using the back of the ladle, spread the batter in a circular motion to form a thick pancake.
    - Sprinkle any desired toppings (onions, tomatoes, green chilies, coriander leaves, etc.) evenly over the Uttapam.
    - Drizzle a little oil or ghee around the edges of the Uttapam and in the center.
    - Sprinkle any desired spices (optional) like cumin seeds, black mustard seeds, or curry leaves over the Uttapam.
    - Cook the Uttapam for a few minutes on medium-high heat until the bottom turns golden brown and crisp.
    - Once the bottom is cooked, flip the Uttapam using a spatula and cook the other side until it's lightly browned and cooked through.
    - Remove the Uttapam from the tawa and serve hot.
3. Serve:
    - Serve Uttapam hot with coconut chutney, tomato chutney, or any other accompaniment of your choice.

Enjoy your delicious and wholesome Uttapam for breakfast or as a snack!

Medu Vada (Lentil Fritters)

Ingredients:

- 1 cup urad dal (black gram lentils)
- 1-2 green chilies, finely chopped
- 1 tablespoon finely chopped ginger
- 2 tablespoons chopped fresh coriander leaves
- 1 teaspoon whole black peppercorns
- 1 teaspoon cumin seeds
- Salt to taste
- Oil for deep frying

Instructions:

1. Soak the urad dal in water:
    - Rinse the urad dal under cold water until the water runs clear. Soak it in water for 4-6 hours or overnight.
2. Grind the urad dal:
    - Drain the soaked urad dal and transfer it to a blender or wet grinder.
    - Grind the urad dal to a smooth paste, adding very little water if needed. The consistency should be thick and smooth.
3. Add spices and seasonings:
    - Transfer the ground urad dal paste to a large mixing bowl.
    - Add finely chopped green chilies, chopped ginger, chopped coriander leaves, whole black peppercorns, cumin seeds, and salt to taste.
    - Mix all the ingredients together until well combined.
4. Shape the vadas:
    - Heat oil for deep frying in a heavy-bottomed pan or kadai over medium heat.
    - Take a small portion of the batter and shape it into a small ball. Wet your hands with water to prevent sticking.
    - Flatten the ball slightly and make a hole in the center to form a donut shape. You can use your fingers or a wet spoon for this.
5. Fry the vadas:
    - Gently slide the shaped vadas into the hot oil, 2-3 at a time, depending on the size of your frying pan. Be careful not to overcrowd the pan.

- Fry the vadas on medium heat, flipping occasionally, until they turn golden brown and crispy on all sides.
- Remove the fried vadas using a slotted spoon and drain excess oil on paper towels.

6. Serve:
    - Serve hot and crispy Medu Vadas with coconut chutney, sambar (lentil stew), or any other dipping sauce of your choice.

Enjoy your homemade Medu Vadas as a delicious snack or part of a South Indian breakfast spread!

Egg Curry

Ingredients:

- 4 eggs, hard-boiled and peeled
- 2 onions, finely chopped
- 2 tomatoes, finely chopped
- 2-3 green chilies, slit lengthwise
- 1 tablespoon ginger-garlic paste
- 1 teaspoon cumin seeds
- 1 teaspoon coriander powder
- 1/2 teaspoon turmeric powder
- 1/2 teaspoon red chili powder (adjust to taste)
- 1/2 teaspoon garam masala
- Salt to taste
- 2 tablespoons oil
- Fresh coriander leaves for garnish (optional)

Instructions:

1. Heat oil in a pan over medium heat. Add cumin seeds and let them splutter.
2. Add chopped onions and sauté until they turn golden brown.
3. Add ginger-garlic paste and slit green chilies. Sauté for a minute until the raw smell disappears.
4. Add chopped tomatoes and cook until they turn soft and mushy.
5. Add coriander powder, turmeric powder, red chili powder, garam masala, and salt. Mix well and cook for a couple of minutes until the spices are fragrant.
6. Add about a cup of water to the masala mixture and bring it to a gentle simmer.
7. Once the curry base is simmering, gently add the hard-boiled eggs to the pan, ensuring they are submerged in the curry.
8. Allow the curry to simmer for another 5-7 minutes, allowing the flavors to meld together and the eggs to absorb some of the curry's flavors.
9. Taste and adjust the seasoning if needed.
10. Garnish with fresh coriander leaves if using.
11. Serve hot with rice, roti, naan, or any bread of your choice.

Enjoy your flavorful Egg Curry!

Vegetable Cutlet

Ingredients:

- 2 large potatoes, boiled, peeled, and mashed
- 1 cup mixed vegetables (carrots, peas, beans, corn), finely chopped or grated
- 1 small onion, finely chopped
- 2 green chilies, finely chopped (adjust according to spice preference)
- 1-inch piece of ginger, grated
- 2 cloves of garlic, minced
- 1/2 teaspoon cumin seeds
- 1/2 teaspoon turmeric powder
- 1 teaspoon garam masala
- 1 teaspoon coriander powder
- Salt to taste
- 1 tablespoon chopped coriander leaves
- 1 tablespoon lemon juice
- 1 cup breadcrumbs (for coating)
- Oil for shallow frying

Instructions:

1. In a large mixing bowl, combine the mashed potatoes, mixed vegetables, chopped onion, green chilies, grated ginger, minced garlic, cumin seeds, turmeric powder, garam masala, coriander powder, salt, chopped coriander leaves, and lemon juice. Mix everything together until well combined.
2. Divide the mixture into equal-sized portions and shape each portion into a flat round or oval shape, resembling cutlets.
3. Spread the breadcrumbs on a plate. Gently coat each cutlet with breadcrumbs, pressing lightly to ensure they adhere to the surface of the cutlets.
4. Heat oil in a non-stick skillet or frying pan over medium heat.
5. Once the oil is hot, carefully place the coated cutlets in the pan, ensuring they don't overlap.
6. Shallow fry the cutlets until golden brown and crispy on one side, then carefully flip them over and fry the other side until golden brown and crispy.
7. Once both sides are evenly cooked and crispy, remove the cutlets from the pan and drain excess oil on paper towels.

8. Serve the vegetable cutlets hot with ketchup, mint chutney, or any dipping sauce of your choice.

Enjoy your delicious and crunchy vegetable cutlets as a snack or appetizer!

Paneer Bhurji (Scrambled Cottage Cheese)

Ingredients:

- 200 grams paneer (cottage cheese), crumbled
- 1 large onion, finely chopped
- 2 tomatoes, finely chopped
- 2 green chilies, finely chopped (adjust according to spice preference)
- 1 tablespoon ginger-garlic paste
- 1/2 teaspoon cumin seeds
- 1/2 teaspoon turmeric powder
- 1 teaspoon red chili powder (adjust to taste)
- 1 teaspoon coriander powder
- 1/2 teaspoon garam masala
- Salt to taste
- 2 tablespoons oil or ghee
- Fresh coriander leaves for garnish (optional)

Instructions:

1. Heat oil or ghee in a pan or skillet over medium heat.
2. Add cumin seeds and let them splutter.
3. Add chopped onions and sauté until they turn golden brown.
4. Add ginger-garlic paste and chopped green chilies. Sauté for a minute until the raw smell disappears.
5. Add chopped tomatoes and cook until they turn soft and mushy.
6. Add turmeric powder, red chili powder, coriander powder, garam masala, and salt. Mix well and cook for a couple of minutes until the spices are fragrant and the oil starts to separate from the masala.
7. Add crumbled paneer to the pan and mix gently with the masala until well combined. Cook for another 2-3 minutes, stirring occasionally, allowing the paneer to absorb the flavors of the spices.
8. Garnish with freshly chopped coriander leaves if using.
9. Serve hot Paneer Bhurji with roti, paratha, or any bread of your choice.

Enjoy your flavorful and aromatic Paneer Bhurji!

Bread Pakora (Spiced Bread Fritters)

Ingredients:

For Potato Filling:

- 2 large potatoes, boiled, peeled, and mashed
- 1 small onion, finely chopped
- 1 green chili, finely chopped (adjust according to spice preference)
- 1/2 teaspoon cumin seeds
- 1/2 teaspoon turmeric powder
- 1 teaspoon red chili powder (adjust to taste)
- 1 teaspoon coriander powder
- Salt to taste
- 1 tablespoon chopped coriander leaves
- Oil for sautéing

For Bread Pakora:

- 8 slices of bread (white or whole wheat)
- Chickpea flour (besan) for batter
- Water, as needed for batter
- 1/2 teaspoon carom seeds (ajwain)
- Salt to taste
- 1/2 teaspoon turmeric powder
- Oil for deep frying

Instructions:

1. Prepare Potato Filling:
    - Heat oil in a pan over medium heat.
    - Add cumin seeds and let them splutter.
    - Add chopped onions and sauté until they turn translucent.
    - Add chopped green chili and sauté for a minute.
    - Add mashed potatoes, turmeric powder, red chili powder, coriander powder, salt, and chopped coriander leaves. Mix well and cook for 2-3 minutes. The filling should be dry. Remove from heat and let it cool.

2. Prepare Bread Pakora Assembly:
   - Trim the edges of the bread slices (optional).
   - Place a spoonful of the prepared potato filling on one slice of bread and spread it evenly.
   - Cover the filling with another slice of bread to make a sandwich. Press gently to seal the edges.
3. Prepare Chickpea Flour Batter:
   - In a bowl, add chickpea flour, carom seeds, turmeric powder, and salt. Mix well.
   - Gradually add water to the chickpea flour mixture, whisking continuously, until you get a smooth batter with a thick pouring consistency. Ensure there are no lumps in the batter.
4. Dip and Fry Bread Pakoras:
   - Heat oil in a deep frying pan or kadai over medium-high heat.
   - Once the oil is hot, dip each prepared bread sandwich into the chickpea flour batter, ensuring it's coated evenly on all sides.
   - Gently place the coated bread pakora into the hot oil and fry until golden brown and crispy on both sides, turning occasionally. Fry in batches, if necessary, ensuring not to overcrowd the pan.
   - Once done, remove the fried bread pakoras using a slotted spoon and drain excess oil on paper towels.
5. Serve:
   - Serve hot and crispy Bread Pakoras with green chutney, tamarind chutney, or ketchup.

Enjoy your delicious and crunchy Bread Pakoras as a tasty snack or appetizer!

Aloo Tikki (Potato Patties)

Ingredients:

- 4 large potatoes, boiled, peeled, and mashed
- 1 small onion, finely chopped
- 2 green chilies, finely chopped (adjust according to spice preference)
- 1 teaspoon ginger paste or grated ginger
- 1 teaspoon cumin seeds
- 1 teaspoon coriander powder
- 1/2 teaspoon red chili powder (adjust to taste)
- 1/2 teaspoon garam masala
- Salt to taste
- 2 tablespoons chopped fresh coriander leaves
- 2 tablespoons corn flour or chickpea flour (besan)
- Oil for shallow frying

Instructions:

1. In a large mixing bowl, combine the mashed potatoes, chopped onion, chopped green chilies, ginger paste, cumin seeds, coriander powder, red chili powder, garam masala, salt, and chopped fresh coriander leaves. Mix well until all the ingredients are evenly distributed.
2. Add corn flour or chickpea flour to the potato mixture. This helps bind the ingredients together and makes the tikkis crispy. Mix well to form a smooth dough-like mixture.
3. Divide the potato mixture into equal-sized portions and shape each portion into a round or oval-shaped patty. You can flatten them slightly with your palms.
4. Heat oil in a non-stick skillet or frying pan over medium heat for shallow frying.
5. Once the oil is hot, carefully place the shaped potato patties into the pan, ensuring they don't overlap.
6. Shallow fry the tikkis until golden brown and crispy on one side, then carefully flip them over and fry the other side until golden brown and crispy.
7. Once both sides are evenly cooked and crispy, remove the tikkis from the pan and place them on a plate lined with paper towels to absorb excess oil.
8. Serve hot Aloo Tikki with green chutney, tamarind chutney, yogurt, or ketchup. You can also serve them with chole (chickpea curry) to make Aloo Tikki Chaat.

Enjoy your homemade Aloo Tikki as a delicious snack or appetizer!

Dhokla (Steamed Chickpea Flour Cake)

Ingredients:

For Dhokla Batter:

- 1 cup chickpea flour (besan)
- 1/4 cup semolina (sooji)
- 1/2 cup yogurt (curd)
- 1 teaspoon ginger paste
- 1 green chili, finely chopped (adjust according to spice preference)
- 1/2 teaspoon turmeric powder
- 1 teaspoon sugar
- Salt to taste
- 1 teaspoon fruit salt (eno) or 1/2 teaspoon baking soda
- 1 tablespoon lemon juice
- 1 tablespoon oil

For Tempering:

- 2 tablespoons oil
- 1 teaspoon mustard seeds
- 1 teaspoon cumin seeds
- 2-3 green chilies, slit lengthwise
- 8-10 curry leaves
- 2 tablespoons chopped coriander leaves
- 1 tablespoon grated coconut (optional)
- 2 tablespoons water
- 1 tablespoon sugar
- 1 tablespoon lemon juice
- Salt to taste

Instructions:

1. Prepare Dhokla Batter:
    - In a large mixing bowl, combine chickpea flour, semolina, yogurt, ginger paste, chopped green chili, turmeric powder, sugar, salt, and oil.

- Mix well to form a smooth batter. Add water as needed to achieve a pouring consistency similar to pancake batter.
- Let the batter rest for 10-15 minutes to allow the semolina to absorb the moisture.

2. Prepare Steamer:
   - Meanwhile, grease a steaming plate or dhokla tray with oil.
3. Add Fruit Salt or Baking Soda:
   - After the resting period, add fruit salt or baking soda to the batter along with lemon juice.
   - Mix gently until the batter becomes frothy.
4. Steam Dhokla:
   - Immediately pour the batter into the greased steaming plate or dhokla tray.
   - Place the steaming plate or tray in a steamer or a large pot filled with water.
   - Steam the dhokla on high heat for about 12-15 minutes or until a toothpick inserted into the center comes out clean.
5. Prepare Tempering:
   - Heat oil in a small pan over medium heat for tempering.
   - Add mustard seeds and cumin seeds. Let them splutter.
   - Add slit green chilies and curry leaves. Saute for a few seconds.
   - Add water, sugar, lemon juice, and salt. Mix well and bring the mixture to a boil.
   - Turn off the heat and pour the tempering evenly over the steamed dhokla.
6. Garnish:
   - Garnish the dhokla with chopped coriander leaves and grated coconut (if using).
7. Serve:
   - Allow the dhokla to cool for a few minutes, then cut it into square or diamond-shaped pieces.
   - Serve the dhokla warm or at room temperature with green chutney or tamarind chutney.

Enjoy your homemade Dhokla as a light and flavorful snack or breakfast dish!

Sabudana Khichdi (Tapioca Pearl Pilaf)

Ingredients:

- 1 cup sabudana (tapioca pearls)
- 2 medium-sized potatoes, peeled and diced
- 1/2 cup roasted peanuts, coarsely ground
- 2-3 green chilies, finely chopped (adjust according to spice preference)
- 1 teaspoon cumin seeds
- 2 tablespoons ghee or oil
- 1 teaspoon sugar (optional)
- Salt to taste
- Fresh coriander leaves for garnish (optional)
- Lemon wedges for serving (optional)

Instructions:

1. Rinse and Soak Sabudana:
    - Rinse the sabudana under cold water until the water runs clear.
    - Transfer the rinsed sabudana to a bowl and add enough water to soak them completely. Let them soak for 4-5 hours or overnight. The sabudana should swell up and become soft.
2. Prepare Potatoes:
    - Peel the potatoes and dice them into small cubes.
    - Heat ghee or oil in a pan over medium heat.
    - Add the diced potatoes to the pan and sauté until they are cooked through and lightly golden brown. Remove them from the pan and set aside.
3. Temper and Cook:
    - In the same pan, heat ghee or oil over medium heat.
    - Add cumin seeds and let them splutter.
    - Add chopped green chilies and sauté for a few seconds.
    - Add the soaked sabudana to the pan, along with roasted peanuts, cooked potatoes, sugar (if using), and salt to taste.
    - Mix everything well and cook for 4-5 minutes, stirring occasionally, until the sabudana pearls become translucent and soft. Be gentle while stirring to prevent them from sticking to the bottom of the pan.
4. Garnish and Serve:

- Once the sabudana khichdi is cooked, turn off the heat.
- Garnish with chopped coriander leaves, if using.
- Serve hot sabudana khichdi with lemon wedges on the side for squeezing over the khichdi before eating.

Enjoy your flavorful and comforting Sabudana Khichdi as a delicious breakfast or fasting dish!

Chana Masala (Spiced Chickpeas)

Ingredients:

- 2 cups dried chickpeas, soaked overnight or for at least 8 hours (or you can use 3 cans of cooked chickpeas, drained and rinsed)
- 2 tablespoons oil or ghee
- 1 large onion, finely chopped
- 2-3 green chilies, slit lengthwise (adjust according to spice preference)
- 1 tablespoon ginger-garlic paste
- 2 medium-sized tomatoes, finely chopped or blended into a puree
- 2 teaspoons ground coriander
- 1 teaspoon ground cumin
- 1/2 teaspoon turmeric powder
- 1/2 teaspoon red chili powder (adjust to taste)
- 1 teaspoon garam masala
- Salt to taste
- 1 tablespoon dried fenugreek leaves (kasuri methi), crushed (optional)
- 2 tablespoons chopped fresh coriander leaves for garnish (optional)
- Lemon wedges for serving (optional)

Instructions:

1. If using dried chickpeas, drain and rinse them after soaking. If using canned chickpeas, drain and rinse them before using.
2. Heat oil or ghee in a large pot or pressure cooker over medium heat. Add chopped onions and sauté until they turn golden brown.
3. Add slit green chilies and ginger-garlic paste to the pot. Sauté for a minute until the raw smell disappears.
4. Add chopped tomatoes or tomato puree to the pot. Cook until the tomatoes are soft and the oil starts to separate from the masala.
5. Add ground coriander, ground cumin, turmeric powder, red chili powder, garam masala, and salt to the pot. Mix well and cook for a couple of minutes until the spices are fragrant.
6. Add the soaked or canned chickpeas to the pot along with enough water to cover them. Bring the mixture to a boil.

7. Once boiling, reduce the heat to low, cover the pot, and let the chickpeas simmer for 20-25 minutes, or until they are tender and cooked through. If using a pressure cooker, cook for about 5-6 whistles.
8. Once the chickpeas are cooked, check the consistency of the gravy. If it's too thick, add more water as needed. If it's too thin, let it simmer uncovered until it reaches your desired consistency.
9. Optional step: Add crushed dried fenugreek leaves (kasuri methi) to the pot for extra flavor. Mix well.
10. Garnish the Chana Masala with chopped fresh coriander leaves, if using.
11. Serve hot Chana Masala with rice, roti, naan, or any bread of your choice. You can also serve it with lemon wedges on the side for squeezing over the curry before eating.

Enjoy your delicious and flavorful Chana Masala!

Poori Bhaji (Fried Bread with Potato Curry)

Ingredients:

For Poori:

- 2 cups whole wheat flour (atta)
- Water, as needed
- Salt to taste
- Oil for deep frying

For Potato Bhaji:

- 4-5 medium-sized potatoes, boiled, peeled, and mashed
- 1 tablespoon oil
- 1 teaspoon mustard seeds
- 1 teaspoon cumin seeds
- 1 onion, finely chopped
- 2 green chilies, finely chopped (adjust according to spice preference)
- 1 teaspoon ginger-garlic paste
- 1/2 teaspoon turmeric powder
- 1 teaspoon red chili powder (adjust to taste)
- 1 teaspoon coriander powder
- 1/2 teaspoon garam masala
- Salt to taste
- Fresh coriander leaves for garnish (optional)
- Lemon wedges for serving (optional)

Instructions:

1. Prepare the Potato Bhaji:
    - Heat oil in a pan over medium heat.
    - Add mustard seeds and cumin seeds. Let them splutter.
    - Add chopped onions and sauté until they turn translucent.

- Add chopped green chilies and ginger-garlic paste. Sauté for a minute until the raw smell disappears.
- Add turmeric powder, red chili powder, coriander powder, garam masala, and salt. Mix well.
- Add mashed potatoes to the pan and mix until the spices are evenly coated. Cook for 3-4 minutes, stirring occasionally. If the mixture is too dry, you can add a little water to adjust the consistency.
- Garnish with chopped fresh coriander leaves, if using. Keep the potato bhaji warm while you prepare the pooris.

2. Prepare the Poori Dough:
    - In a large mixing bowl, combine whole wheat flour and salt.
    - Gradually add water and knead the dough until it's smooth and soft. The dough should be firm but pliable.
    - Cover the dough with a damp cloth and let it rest for about 15-20 minutes.

3. Shape and Fry the Pooris:
    - Divide the dough into small lemon-sized balls.
    - Roll each ball into a small disc (poori) using a rolling pin. The pooris should be about 3-4 inches in diameter.
    - Heat oil in a deep frying pan or kadai over medium heat for deep frying.
    - Once the oil is hot, carefully slide one poori at a time into the hot oil.
    - Gently press down on the poori with a slotted spoon to help it puff up.
    - Fry the poori until it puffs up and turns golden brown on both sides.
    - Remove the fried poori from the oil using a slotted spoon and drain excess oil on paper towels.
    - Repeat the process with the remaining dough balls.

4. Serve:
    - Serve hot Poori Bhaji with the prepared potato bhaji.
    - Optionally, serve with lemon wedges on the side for squeezing over the bhaji before eating.

Enjoy your delicious and comforting Poori Bhaji for breakfast or brunch!

Masala Dosa

Ingredients:

For Dosa Batter:

- 1 cup parboiled rice
- 1/2 cup split urad dal (black gram lentils)
- 1/4 teaspoon fenugreek seeds (methi seeds)
- Water, as needed
- Salt to taste

For Potato Filling (Masala):

- 3-4 large potatoes, boiled, peeled, and mashed
- 1 tablespoon oil
- 1 teaspoon mustard seeds
- 1 teaspoon cumin seeds
- 1 onion, finely chopped
- 2 green chilies, finely chopped (adjust according to spice preference)
- 1 teaspoon ginger-garlic paste
- 1/2 teaspoon turmeric powder
- 1 teaspoon red chili powder (adjust to taste)
- 1 teaspoon coriander powder
- 1/2 teaspoon garam masala
- Salt to taste
- Fresh coriander leaves for garnish (optional)

For Making Dosa:

- Dosa batter (prepared in advance)
- Oil or ghee for cooking dosas

Instructions:

1. Prepare Dosa Batter:
    - Rinse the rice and urad dal separately under cold water until the water runs clear. Soak them in water separately, along with fenugreek seeds, for at least 4-6 hours.
    - After soaking, drain the water from the rice and urad dal.
    - Grind the urad dal in a blender or wet grinder with enough water to make a smooth and fluffy batter. The consistency should be thick and airy. Transfer the batter to a large bowl.
    - Grind the soaked rice in the same blender or wet grinder, adding water gradually to make a smooth batter. The consistency should be slightly coarse compared to the urad dal batter.
    - Combine the rice batter with the urad dal batter in the large bowl. Mix well using your hands or a spoon until thoroughly combined.
    - Add salt to the batter and mix again. The batter should have a thick pouring consistency.
    - Cover the bowl with a lid or cloth and let the batter ferment in a warm place for 8-12 hours or overnight. During fermentation, the batter will rise and double in volume.
2. Prepare Potato Filling (Masala):
    - Heat oil in a pan over medium heat.
    - Add mustard seeds and cumin seeds. Let them splutter.
    - Add chopped onions and sauté until they turn translucent.
    - Add chopped green chilies and ginger-garlic paste. Sauté for a minute until the raw smell disappears.
    - Add turmeric powder, red chili powder, coriander powder, garam masala, and salt. Mix well.
    - Add mashed potatoes to the pan and mix until the spices are evenly coated. Cook for 3-4 minutes, stirring occasionally. If the mixture is too dry, you can add a little water to adjust the consistency.
    - Garnish with chopped fresh coriander leaves, if using. Keep the potato filling warm while you prepare the dosas.
3. Make Masala Dosa:
    - Heat a non-stick dosa tawa or skillet over medium heat.
    - Pour a ladleful of dosa batter onto the center of the tawa.
    - Using the back of the ladle, spread the batter in a circular motion to form a thin, even crepe.
    - Drizzle a little oil or ghee around the edges of the dosa and in the center.
    - Once the edges start to lift and crisp up, spoon some of the prepared potato filling (masala) onto the center of the dosa.

- Fold the dosa over the filling to form a semi-circle or roll it into a cylindrical shape.
- Cook the dosa for a few more minutes until it turns golden brown and crispy on both sides.
- Repeat the process with the remaining dosa batter and potato filling.

4. Serve:
   - Serve hot Masala Dosas with coconut chutney, tomato chutney, or sambar (lentil stew).

Enjoy your delicious and flavorful Masala Dosas for breakfast or as a snack!

Egg Bhurji (Scrambled Eggs)

Ingredients:

- 4 eggs
- 1 tablespoon oil or ghee
- 1 onion, finely chopped
- 1 tomato, finely chopped
- 2 green chilies, finely chopped (adjust according to spice preference)
- 1 teaspoon ginger-garlic paste
- 1/2 teaspoon cumin seeds
- 1/2 teaspoon turmeric powder
- 1 teaspoon red chili powder (adjust to taste)
- 1/2 teaspoon garam masala
- Salt to taste
- Fresh coriander leaves for garnish (optional)

Instructions:

1. Heat oil or ghee in a pan over medium heat.
2. Add cumin seeds and let them splutter.
3. Add finely chopped onions and sauté until they turn translucent.
4. Add ginger-garlic paste and chopped green chilies. Sauté for a minute until the raw smell disappears.
5. Add chopped tomatoes to the pan and cook until they turn soft and mushy.
6. Add turmeric powder, red chili powder, garam masala, and salt to taste. Mix well and cook for a couple of minutes until the spices are fragrant and the oil starts to separate from the masala.
7. Crack the eggs directly into the pan. Use a spatula to break the eggs and scramble them with the masala mixture.
8. Cook the eggs, stirring occasionally, until they are fully cooked and no longer runny.
9. Garnish with chopped fresh coriander leaves, if using.
10. Serve hot Egg Bhurji with roti, paratha, or bread of your choice. You can also serve it as a side dish with rice.

Enjoy your delicious and comforting Egg Bhurji!

Rava Upma (Semolina Breakfast Porridge)

Ingredients:

- 1 cup semolina (rava or sooji)
- 2 tablespoons oil or ghee
- 1 teaspoon mustard seeds
- 1 teaspoon cumin seeds
- 1/2 teaspoon urad dal (split black gram lentils)
- 1/2 teaspoon chana dal (split chickpeas)
- 1 onion, finely chopped
- 1 green chili, finely chopped (adjust according to spice preference)
- 1-inch piece of ginger, finely chopped
- 8-10 curry leaves
- 2-3 cups water
- Salt to taste
- Fresh coriander leaves for garnish (optional)
- Lemon wedges for serving (optional)

Instructions:

1. Dry roast the Semolina:
    - Heat a heavy-bottomed pan or kadai over medium heat.
    - Add the semolina to the pan and dry roast it for 4-5 minutes, stirring continuously, until it turns light golden brown and aromatic. Be careful not to burn it. Transfer the roasted semolina to a plate and set aside.
2. Prepare the Tempering:
    - In the same pan, heat oil or ghee over medium heat.
    - Add mustard seeds and let them splutter.
    - Add cumin seeds, urad dal, and chana dal. Sauté until the dals turn golden brown.
    - Add chopped onions, green chilies, and chopped ginger. Sauté until the onions turn translucent.
3. Cook the Vegetables:
    - Add curry leaves to the pan and sauté for a few seconds.

- Add any vegetables of your choice, such as finely chopped carrots, peas, bell peppers, or beans. Sauté for 2-3 minutes until the vegetables are slightly cooked.

4. Add Semolina and Water:
    - Reduce the heat to low and slowly add the roasted semolina to the pan while stirring continuously to prevent lumps from forming.
    - Immediately pour water into the pan while stirring continuously. Be careful as the mixture will splutter.
    - Add salt to taste and mix well.
5. Cook the Upma:
    - Cover the pan with a lid and let the upma cook on low heat for 3-4 minutes, allowing the semolina to absorb the water and cook through.
    - Stir occasionally to prevent sticking and ensure even cooking. If the upma becomes too thick, you can add a little more water.
    - Once the semolina is cooked and the water is absorbed, remove the pan from the heat.
6. Garnish and Serve:
    - Garnish the Rava Upma with freshly chopped coriander leaves, if using.
    - Serve hot Rava Upma with coconut chutney, pickle, or yogurt on the side. You can also serve it with lemon wedges for squeezing over the upma before eating.

Enjoy your warm and comforting Rava Upma for breakfast or as a light meal!

Aloo Puri (Potato Stuffed Fried Bread)

Ingredients:

For Puri Dough:

- 2 cups whole wheat flour (atta)
- Water, as needed
- Salt to taste
- Oil for deep frying

For Potato Filling:

- 4 medium-sized potatoes, boiled, peeled, and mashed
- 1 tablespoon oil
- 1 teaspoon cumin seeds
- 1 teaspoon mustard seeds
- 1 onion, finely chopped
- 2 green chilies, finely chopped (adjust according to spice preference)
- 1 teaspoon ginger-garlic paste
- 1/2 teaspoon turmeric powder
- 1 teaspoon red chili powder (adjust to taste)
- 1 teaspoon coriander powder
- 1/2 teaspoon garam masala
- Salt to taste
- Fresh coriander leaves for garnish (optional)

Instructions:

1. Prepare the Potato Filling:
    - Heat oil in a pan over medium heat.
    - Add cumin seeds and mustard seeds. Let them splutter.
    - Add chopped onions and sauté until they turn translucent.
    - Add chopped green chilies and ginger-garlic paste. Sauté for a minute until the raw smell disappears.

- Add turmeric powder, red chili powder, coriander powder, garam masala, and salt. Mix well.
- Add mashed potatoes to the pan and mix until the spices are evenly coated. Cook for 3-4 minutes, stirring occasionally. If the mixture is too dry, you can add a little water to adjust the consistency.
- Garnish with chopped fresh coriander leaves, if using. Keep the potato filling warm while you prepare the puris.

2. Prepare the Puri Dough:
   - In a large mixing bowl, combine whole wheat flour and salt.
   - Gradually add water and knead the dough until it's smooth and soft. The dough should be firm but pliable.
   - Cover the dough with a damp cloth and let it rest for about 15-20 minutes.

3. Shape and Fill the Puris:
   - Divide the dough into small lemon-sized balls.
   - Take one dough ball and roll it out into a small disc (puri) using a rolling pin. The puri should be about 3-4 inches in diameter.
   - Place a spoonful of the prepared potato filling onto the center of the puri.
   - Fold the edges of the puri over the filling and seal them to form a stuffed ball. Flatten the stuffed ball slightly with your palms.

4. Fry the Aloo Puris:
   - Heat oil in a deep frying pan or kadai over medium heat for deep frying.
   - Once the oil is hot, carefully slide one stuffed puri at a time into the hot oil.
   - Fry the puris until they turn golden brown and crispy on both sides.
   - Remove the fried puris from the oil using a slotted spoon and drain excess oil on paper towels.
   - Repeat the process with the remaining dough balls and potato filling.

5. Serve:
   - Serve hot Aloo Puris with yogurt, pickle, or any chutney of your choice.

Enjoy your delicious and satisfying Aloo Puris as a special breakfast or snack!

Moong Dal Cheela (Mung Bean Pancakes)

Ingredients:

- 1 cup split yellow moong dal (mung beans), soaked for 4-6 hours
- 1 green chili, chopped (adjust according to spice preference)
- 1-inch piece of ginger, grated
- 1/4 cup chopped fresh coriander leaves
- 1/2 teaspoon cumin seeds
- Salt to taste
- Oil or ghee for cooking

Instructions:

1. Rinse the soaked moong dal under cold water and drain well.
2. In a blender or food processor, add the soaked moong dal along with chopped green chili, grated ginger, chopped coriander leaves, cumin seeds, and salt.
3. Blend the mixture into a smooth batter, adding a little water as needed to achieve a thick pouring consistency. The batter should be smooth and without any coarse grains.
4. Heat a non-stick skillet or dosa tawa over medium heat.
5. Once the skillet is hot, pour a ladleful of the moong dal batter onto the center of the skillet.
6. Using the back of the ladle, spread the batter in a circular motion to form a thin pancake (cheela).
7. Drizzle a little oil or ghee around the edges of the cheela and in the center.
8. Cook the cheela for 2-3 minutes on one side until it turns golden brown and crispy.
9. Flip the cheela over using a spatula and cook for another 1-2 minutes on the other side until golden brown and cooked through.
10. Repeat the process with the remaining batter to make more cheelas.
11. Serve hot Moong Dal Cheelas with chutney, yogurt, or pickle of your choice.

Enjoy your delicious and nutritious Moong Dal Cheelas for breakfast or as a snack!

Kachori (Stuffed Savory Pastry)

Ingredients:

For the Dough:

- 2 cups all-purpose flour (maida)
- 2 tablespoons oil or ghee
- Salt to taste
- Water, as needed

For the Filling:

- 1 cup yellow moong dal (split mung beans), soaked for 4-6 hours
- 2-3 green chilies, chopped (adjust according to spice preference)
- 1 teaspoon ginger, grated
- 1 teaspoon cumin seeds
- 1 teaspoon fennel seeds
- 1/2 teaspoon asafoetida (hing)
- 1/2 teaspoon turmeric powder
- 1 teaspoon red chili powder (adjust to taste)
- 1 teaspoon coriander powder
- 1 teaspoon garam masala
- Salt to taste
- Oil for frying

Instructions:

1. Prepare the Dough:
    - In a large mixing bowl, combine all-purpose flour, salt, and oil or ghee.
    - Mix well using your fingers until the flour resembles breadcrumbs.
    - Gradually add water and knead the mixture into a smooth, firm dough.
    - Cover the dough with a damp cloth and let it rest for 15-20 minutes.
2. Prepare the Filling:
    - Drain the soaked moong dal and rinse it under cold water.

- In a blender or food processor, coarsely grind the moong dal without adding any water. The texture should be coarse, not too fine.
- Heat oil in a pan over medium heat.
- Add cumin seeds and fennel seeds. Let them splutter.
- Add grated ginger, chopped green chilies, and asafoetida. Sauté for a minute.
- Add the coarsely ground moong dal to the pan.
- Add turmeric powder, red chili powder, coriander powder, garam masala, and salt. Mix well.
- Cook the dal mixture for 5-6 minutes, stirring occasionally, until it's cooked through and the moisture evaporates. The filling should be dry. Allow it to cool completely.

3. Shape and Fill the Kachoris:
   - Divide the dough into equal-sized balls.
   - Take one dough ball and roll it out into a small disc (about 3-4 inches in diameter) using a rolling pin.
   - Place a spoonful of the cooled moong dal filling in the center of the disc.
   - Gather the edges of the disc to enclose the filling and seal it properly to form a stuffed ball.
   - Flatten the stuffed ball slightly with your palms.

4. Fry the Kachoris:
   - Heat oil in a deep frying pan or kadai over medium heat for frying.
   - Once the oil is hot, carefully slide one stuffed kachori into the hot oil.
   - Fry the kachori on medium-low heat until it turns golden brown and crispy on both sides.
   - Remove the fried kachori from the oil using a slotted spoon and drain excess oil on paper towels.
   - Repeat the process with the remaining dough balls and filling.

5. Serve:
   - Serve hot and crispy Kachoris with tamarind chutney, green chutney, or yogurt.

Enjoy your delicious and flavorful Kachoris as a snack or appetizer!

Besan Cheela (Chickpea Flour Pancakes)

Ingredients:

- 1 cup chickpea flour (besan)
- 1 onion, finely chopped
- 1 tomato, finely chopped
- 2-3 green chilies, finely chopped (adjust according to spice preference)
- 1/2 inch piece of ginger, grated
- 2 tablespoons chopped fresh coriander leaves
- 1/2 teaspoon cumin seeds
- 1/2 teaspoon turmeric powder
- 1/2 teaspoon red chili powder (adjust to taste)
- Salt to taste
- Water, as needed
- Oil or ghee for cooking

Instructions:

1. In a large mixing bowl, combine chickpea flour, chopped onions, chopped tomatoes, chopped green chilies, grated ginger, chopped coriander leaves, cumin seeds, turmeric powder, red chili powder, and salt.
2. Gradually add water to the mixture, whisking continuously, until you achieve a smooth batter with a pouring consistency. The batter should not be too thick or too thin.
3. Heat a non-stick skillet or dosa tawa over medium heat.
4. Once the skillet is hot, lightly grease it with oil or ghee.
5. Pour a ladleful of the besan batter onto the center of the skillet.
6. Using the back of the ladle, spread the batter in a circular motion to form a thin pancake (cheela).
7. Drizzle a little oil or ghee around the edges of the cheela and in the center.
8. Cook the cheela for 2-3 minutes on one side until it turns golden brown and crispy.
9. Flip the cheela over using a spatula and cook for another 1-2 minutes on the other side until golden brown and cooked through.
10. Repeat the process with the remaining batter to make more cheelas.
11. Serve hot Besan Cheelas with chutney, yogurt, or pickle of your choice.

Enjoy your delicious and nutritious Besan Cheelas for breakfast, brunch, or as a snack!

Bread Upma (Bread Stir-fry)

Ingredients:

- 4-5 slices of bread, preferably slightly stale or leftover bread, cut into small pieces
- 2 tablespoons oil or ghee
- 1 teaspoon mustard seeds
- 1 teaspoon cumin seeds
- 1 onion, finely chopped
- 1 green chili, finely chopped (adjust according to spice preference)
- 1/2 inch piece of ginger, grated
- 1-2 sprigs of curry leaves
- 1 carrot, finely chopped
- 1 small capsicum (bell pepper), finely chopped
- 1/2 cup green peas (fresh or frozen)
- 1/2 teaspoon turmeric powder
- 1 teaspoon red chili powder (adjust to taste)
- Salt to taste
- Fresh coriander leaves for garnish (optional)
- Lemon wedges for serving (optional)

Instructions:

1. Heat oil or ghee in a pan over medium heat.
2. Add mustard seeds and cumin seeds. Let them splutter.
3. Add chopped onions and sauté until they turn translucent.
4. Add chopped green chili, grated ginger, and curry leaves. Sauté for a minute until fragrant.
5. Add chopped carrots, capsicum, and green peas to the pan. Cook for 3-4 minutes until the vegetables are slightly tender.
6. Add turmeric powder, red chili powder, and salt to taste. Mix well.
7. Add the bread pieces to the pan. Gently toss and mix until the bread is coated with the spices and vegetables.
8. Cook for another 3-4 minutes, stirring occasionally, until the bread is heated through and slightly crispy.
9. Garnish with freshly chopped coriander leaves, if using.

10. Serve hot Bread Upma with lemon wedges on the side for squeezing over the upma before eating.

Enjoy your flavorful and comforting Bread Upma for breakfast or as a light meal!

Matar Kulcha (Peas Curry with Flatbread)

Ingredients:

For Matar (Peas) Curry:

- 2 cups green peas (fresh or frozen)
- 2 tablespoons oil
- 1 teaspoon cumin seeds
- 1 onion, finely chopped
- 2 tomatoes, finely chopped
- 2 green chilies, finely chopped (adjust according to spice preference)
- 1 tablespoon ginger-garlic paste
- 1 teaspoon coriander powder
- 1/2 teaspoon turmeric powder
- 1/2 teaspoon red chili powder (adjust to taste)
- 1/2 teaspoon garam masala
- Salt to taste
- Fresh coriander leaves for garnish (optional)
- Lemon wedges for serving (optional)

For Kulcha:

- 2 cups all-purpose flour (maida)
- 1/2 cup yogurt
- 1 teaspoon baking powder
- 1/2 teaspoon baking soda
- 1/2 teaspoon sugar
- 1/4 cup oil or ghee
- Water, as needed
- Butter or ghee for brushing (optional)

Instructions:

1. Prepare the Matar (Peas) Curry:
    - Heat oil in a pan over medium heat.
    - Add cumin seeds and let them splutter.

- Add chopped onions and sauté until they turn translucent.
- Add chopped green chilies and ginger-garlic paste. Sauté for a minute until the raw smell disappears.
- Add chopped tomatoes to the pan and cook until they turn soft and mushy.
- Add coriander powder, turmeric powder, red chili powder, garam masala, and salt. Mix well and cook for a couple of minutes until the spices are fragrant and the oil starts to separate from the masala.
- Add green peas to the pan and mix well.
- Add a little water if needed to adjust the consistency of the curry. Cover the pan and let the peas cook for 5-7 minutes until they are tender and cooked through.
- Garnish with freshly chopped coriander leaves, if using.

2. Prepare the Kulcha:
    - In a large mixing bowl, combine all-purpose flour, yogurt, baking powder, baking soda, sugar, and oil or ghee.
    - Mix well and knead into a soft and smooth dough, adding water as needed.
    - Cover the dough with a damp cloth and let it rest for about 1-2 hours.
    - After resting, divide the dough into equal-sized balls.
    - Roll out each dough ball into a small disc (kulcha) using a rolling pin.
    - Heat a tawa or skillet over medium heat.
    - Place the rolled kulcha on the hot tawa and cook for a minute on one side until bubbles start to appear.
    - Flip the kulcha over and cook for another minute on the other side until it puffs up and turns golden brown.
    - Repeat the process with the remaining dough balls to make more kulchas.

3. Serve:
    - Serve hot Matar Kulcha, garnished with fresh coriander leaves and accompanied by lemon wedges.
    - Optionally, brush the kulchas with butter or ghee before serving for extra flavor.

Enjoy your delicious and flavorful Matar Kulcha as a street-style snack or meal!

Egg Roll

Ingredients:

For the Egg Rolls:

- 4 large eggs
- Salt and pepper to taste
- 4 large flour tortillas or egg roll wrappers
- 1 tablespoon oil or butter for cooking

For the Filling (Optional, Customize as Desired):

- Thinly sliced vegetables (such as bell peppers, onions, carrots, cabbage, mushrooms)
- Cooked protein (such as shredded chicken, cooked shrimp, or tofu)
- Cheese (such as shredded cheddar or mozzarella)

For Serving (Optional):

- Sriracha sauce, sweet chili sauce, or your favorite dipping sauce

Instructions:

1. Prepare the Filling (Optional):
    - Heat a tablespoon of oil in a pan over medium-high heat.
    - Add thinly sliced vegetables and cook until they are tender-crisp, about 3-4 minutes.
    - If using cooked protein, add it to the pan and cook until heated through.
    - Season with salt and pepper to taste. Set aside.
2. Cook the Eggs:
    - In a bowl, beat the eggs and season with salt and pepper.
    - Heat a non-stick skillet over medium heat and add a little oil or butter.

- Pour a quarter of the beaten eggs into the skillet, tilting it to spread the egg evenly into a thin layer.
- Cook the egg for 1-2 minutes until it sets on the bottom.
- Using a spatula, carefully flip the egg and cook for another 1-2 minutes until cooked through.
- Remove the cooked egg from the skillet and repeat the process with the remaining beaten eggs.

3. Assemble the Egg Rolls:
   - Place a cooked egg on a flour tortilla or egg roll wrapper.
   - Add a portion of the cooked vegetable filling (if using) on top of the egg.
   - Add cheese (if using) on top of the vegetables.
4. Roll the Egg Rolls:
   - Fold the sides of the tortilla or wrapper over the filling.
   - Roll up tightly from the bottom to form a cylinder-shaped roll.
5. Cook the Egg Rolls:
   - Heat a skillet or griddle over medium heat.
   - Add a little oil or butter to the skillet.
   - Place the rolled egg rolls seam-side down on the skillet.
   - Cook for 2-3 minutes on each side until golden brown and crispy.
6. Serve:
   - Remove the cooked egg rolls from the skillet and let them cool slightly.
   - Slice the egg rolls diagonally into halves or thirds.
   - Serve hot with your favorite dipping sauce, such as sriracha sauce or sweet chili sauce.

Enjoy your delicious homemade egg rolls as a snack or light meal! You can also customize the fillings according to your preferences.

Methi Thepla (Fenugreek Flatbread)

Ingredients:

- 2 cups whole wheat flour (atta)
- 1 cup fresh fenugreek leaves (methi), washed and finely chopped
- 1/4 cup yogurt
- 1 tablespoon oil
- 1 teaspoon ginger-green chili paste
- 1/2 teaspoon turmeric powder
- 1 teaspoon red chili powder (adjust to taste)
- 1/2 teaspoon cumin seeds
- 1/2 teaspoon coriander powder
- Salt to taste
- Oil or ghee for cooking the theplas
- Water, as needed

Instructions:

1. In a large mixing bowl, combine whole wheat flour, chopped fenugreek leaves, yogurt, oil, ginger-green chili paste, turmeric powder, red chili powder, cumin seeds, coriander powder, and salt.
2. Mix well to incorporate all the ingredients.
3. Gradually add water as needed and knead the mixture into a smooth, soft dough. The dough should be firm yet pliable.
4. Cover the dough with a damp cloth and let it rest for about 15-20 minutes.
5. After resting, divide the dough into equal-sized balls.
6. Take one dough ball and flatten it between your palms to form a small disc.
7. Dust the disc with some flour and roll it out into a thin circle, about 6-7 inches in diameter, using a rolling pin.
8. Heat a tawa or skillet over medium heat.
9. Place the rolled thepla onto the hot tawa and let it cook for about 1 minute on one side until small bubbles start to appear.
10. Flip the thepla over and drizzle a little oil or ghee on top.
11. Cook for another 1-2 minutes on the other side until golden brown spots appear and the thepla is cooked through.
12. Remove the cooked thepla from the tawa and transfer it to a plate.

13. Repeat the process with the remaining dough balls to make more theplas.
14. Serve hot Methi Theplas with yogurt, pickle, or any chutney of your choice.

Enjoy your delicious and nutritious Methi Theplas as a wholesome meal or snack! They can be stored in an airtight container and enjoyed later as well.

Vegetable Uttapam

Ingredients:

For the Uttapam Batter:

- 1 cup rice (any variety, preferably parboiled)
- 1/2 cup urad dal (split black gram lentils)
- 1/4 cup chana dal (split chickpeas)
- 1/2 teaspoon fenugreek seeds (methi seeds)
- Salt to taste
- Water, as needed

For the Vegetable Topping:

- 1 onion, finely chopped
- 1 tomato, finely chopped
- 1/2 bell pepper (capsicum), finely chopped
- 1/4 cup grated carrot
- 2-3 green chilies, finely chopped (adjust according to spice preference)
- 2 tablespoons chopped fresh coriander leaves
- Salt to taste

For Cooking:

- Oil or ghee for cooking the uttapam

Instructions:

1. Prepare the Uttapam Batter:
    - Rinse rice, urad dal, chana dal, and fenugreek seeds together under cold water.
    - Soak them in water separately for 4-6 hours or overnight.
    - Drain the soaked ingredients and transfer them to a blender or wet grinder.

- Grind into a smooth batter, adding water as needed. The consistency should be similar to pancake batter.
- Transfer the batter to a large bowl, add salt, and mix well.
- Allow the batter to ferment for 8-10 hours or overnight in a warm place. The fermentation process gives uttapam its characteristic tangy flavor and fluffy texture.

2. Prepare the Vegetable Topping:
    - In a bowl, mix together chopped onions, tomatoes, bell peppers, grated carrots, chopped green chilies, and coriander leaves.
    - Add salt to taste and mix well. Set aside.

3. Make Vegetable Uttapam:
    - Heat a non-stick skillet or griddle over medium heat.
    - Once the skillet is hot, pour a ladleful of the fermented uttapam batter onto the center of the skillet.
    - Using the back of the ladle, spread the batter into a thick circle, about 6-7 inches in diameter.
    - Sprinkle a generous amount of the prepared vegetable topping evenly over the surface of the uttapam.
    - Drizzle a little oil or ghee around the edges and on top of the vegetables.
    - Cook the uttapam on medium-low heat for 2-3 minutes until the bottom is golden brown and crispy.
    - Flip the uttapam over using a spatula and cook for another 2-3 minutes on the other side until golden brown and cooked through.
    - Repeat the process with the remaining batter and vegetable topping to make more uttapams.

4. Serve:
    - Serve hot Vegetable Uttapam with coconut chutney, tomato chutney, or sambar.

Enjoy your delicious and nutritious Vegetable Uttapam for breakfast, brunch, or as a light meal!

Anda Bhurji (Indian Style Scrambled Eggs)

Ingredients:

- 4 eggs
- 2 tablespoons oil or ghee
- 1 onion, finely chopped
- 2 tomatoes, finely chopped
- 2 green chilies, finely chopped (adjust according to spice preference)
- 1 teaspoon ginger-garlic paste
- 1/2 teaspoon cumin seeds
- 1/2 teaspoon turmeric powder
- 1 teaspoon red chili powder (adjust to taste)
- 1/2 teaspoon garam masala
- Salt to taste
- Fresh coriander leaves for garnish (optional)

Instructions:

1. Heat oil or ghee in a pan over medium heat.
2. Add cumin seeds and let them splutter.
3. Add finely chopped onions and sauté until they turn translucent.
4. Add ginger-garlic paste and chopped green chilies. Sauté for a minute until the raw smell disappears.
5. Add chopped tomatoes to the pan and cook until they turn soft and mushy.
6. Add turmeric powder, red chili powder, garam masala, and salt to taste. Mix well and cook for a couple of minutes until the spices are fragrant and the oil starts to separate from the masala.
7. Crack the eggs directly into the pan.
8. Using a spatula, break the eggs and scramble them with the masala mixture.
9. Cook the eggs, stirring occasionally, until they are fully cooked and no longer runny.
10. Garnish with freshly chopped coriander leaves, if using.
11. Serve hot Anda Bhurji with roti, paratha, or bread of your choice. You can also serve it as a side dish with rice.

Enjoy your delicious and comforting Anda Bhurji!

Sooji Dhokla (Semolina Steamed Cake)

Ingredients:

For the Dhokla Batter:

- 1 cup semolina (sooji)
- 1/2 cup yogurt (curd)
- 1/2 cup water
- 1 tablespoon oil
- 1 teaspoon mustard seeds
- 1 teaspoon cumin seeds
- 1 teaspoon grated ginger
- 2 green chilies, finely chopped (adjust according to spice preference)
- 1/2 teaspoon turmeric powder
- 1 teaspoon salt, or to taste
- 1 tablespoon lemon juice
- 1 teaspoon baking soda

For Tempering:

- 2 tablespoons oil
- 1 teaspoon mustard seeds
- 1 teaspoon sesame seeds
- 2-3 green chilies, slit lengthwise
- Few curry leaves
- 2 tablespoons chopped coriander leaves for garnish
- Grated coconut for garnish (optional)

Instructions:

1. Prepare the Dhokla Batter:
    - In a mixing bowl, combine semolina, yogurt, and water. Mix well to form a smooth batter without any lumps. Let it rest for 15-20 minutes.
    - Heat oil in a small pan. Add mustard seeds and cumin seeds. Let them crackle.
    - Add grated ginger and chopped green chilies. Sauté for a minute.

- Add this tempering to the semolina batter along with turmeric powder, salt, and lemon juice. Mix well.
- Grease a dhokla plate or a shallow baking dish with oil.

2. Steam the Dhokla:
   - Just before steaming, add baking soda to the batter and mix well. The batter will become frothy.
   - Pour the batter into the greased plate or dish.
   - Heat water in a steamer. Once the water comes to a boil, place the dhokla plate or dish inside the steamer.
   - Cover and steam the dhokla on medium heat for 12-15 minutes or until a toothpick inserted into the center comes out clean.
   - Once steamed, turn off the heat and let the dhokla cool down for a few minutes.

3. Prepare the Tempering:
   - Heat oil in a small pan for tempering.
   - Add mustard seeds and let them crackle.
   - Add sesame seeds, slit green chilies, and curry leaves. Sauté for a minute.
   - Pour this tempering over the steamed dhokla.

4. Serve:
   - Cut the dhokla into squares or diamonds.
   - Garnish with chopped coriander leaves and grated coconut (if using).
   - Serve Sooji Dhokla warm with green chutney or tamarind chutney.

Enjoy your delicious and spongy Sooji Dhokla as a snack or breakfast item!

Palak Paneer Paratha (Spinach Cottage Cheese Stuffed Bread)

Ingredients:

For the Dough:

- 2 cups whole wheat flour (atta)
- Water, as needed
- Salt to taste

For the Filling:

- 1 cup spinach leaves, finely chopped
- 200 grams paneer (cottage cheese), crumbled
- 1 small onion, finely chopped
- 2 green chilies, finely chopped (adjust according to spice preference)
- 1 teaspoon ginger-garlic paste
- 1/2 teaspoon cumin seeds
- 1/2 teaspoon garam masala
- 1/2 teaspoon turmeric powder
- Salt to taste
- Fresh coriander leaves, finely chopped
- Oil or ghee for cooking the parathas

Instructions:

1. Prepare the Dough:
    - In a large mixing bowl, combine whole wheat flour and salt.
    - Gradually add water and knead the mixture into a smooth, soft dough. The dough should be firm but pliable.
    - Cover the dough with a damp cloth and let it rest for about 15-20 minutes.
2. Prepare the Filling:
    - Heat oil in a pan over medium heat.
    - Add cumin seeds and let them splutter.
    - Add finely chopped onions and sauté until they turn translucent.

- Add ginger-garlic paste and chopped green chilies. Sauté for a minute until the raw smell disappears.
- Add finely chopped spinach leaves to the pan and cook until they wilt and release their moisture.
- Add crumbled paneer, garam masala, turmeric powder, and salt to taste. Mix well and cook for 2-3 minutes until the mixture is well combined and any excess moisture evaporates.
- Garnish with freshly chopped coriander leaves. Allow the filling to cool down completely.

3. Assemble and Cook the Parathas:
    - Divide the rested dough into equal-sized balls.
    - Take one dough ball and roll it out into a small disc (about 3-4 inches in diameter) using a rolling pin.
    - Place a spoonful of the prepared spinach-paneer filling onto the center of the disc.
    - Gather the edges of the disc to enclose the filling and seal them properly to form a stuffed ball.
    - Flatten the stuffed ball slightly with your palms.
    - Roll out the stuffed ball gently into a larger disc, ensuring that the filling spreads evenly inside the paratha.
    - Heat a tawa or skillet over medium heat.
    - Place the rolled paratha onto the hot tawa and cook for 1-2 minutes on one side until small bubbles start to appear.
    - Flip the paratha over and drizzle a little oil or ghee on top.
    - Cook for another 1-2 minutes on the other side until golden brown spots appear and the paratha is cooked through.
    - Repeat the process with the remaining dough balls and filling to make more parathas.

4. Serve:
    - Serve hot Palak Paneer Parathas with yogurt, pickle, or any chutney of your choice.

Enjoy your delicious and nutritious Palak Paneer Parathas as a wholesome meal or snack!

Ragi Dosa (Finger Millet Crepes)

Ingredients:

- 1 cup ragi flour (finger millet flour)
- 1/4 cup rice flour
- 1/4 cup urad dal (split black gram lentils)
- Salt to taste
- Water, as needed
- Oil or ghee for cooking the dosas

Instructions:

1. Soak the Urad Dal:
    - Rinse the urad dal under cold water and soak it in water for 4-6 hours or overnight.
2. Prepare the Dosa Batter:
    - After soaking, drain the urad dal and transfer it to a blender or wet grinder.
    - Grind the urad dal into a smooth batter, adding water as needed. The batter should be fluffy and smooth.
    - In a large mixing bowl, combine ragi flour, rice flour, and salt.
    - Add the ground urad dal batter to the dry ingredients and mix well.
    - Gradually add water and mix to form a smooth dosa batter. The consistency should be similar to pancake batter. Let the batter ferment for 6-8 hours or overnight in a warm place. The fermentation process helps in making the dosas light and crispy.
3. Make Ragi Dosas:
    - Heat a non-stick dosa tawa or skillet over medium heat.
    - Once the tawa is hot, pour a ladleful of the dosa batter onto the center of the tawa.
    - Using the back of the ladle, spread the batter in a circular motion to form a thin dosa.
    - Drizzle a little oil or ghee around the edges of the dosa.
    - Cook the dosa on medium heat until the bottom turns golden brown and crispy.
    - Flip the dosa over using a spatula and cook for another minute on the other side until cooked through.

- Repeat the process with the remaining batter to make more dosas.
4. Serve:
    - Serve hot Ragi Dosas with coconut chutney, sambar, or any chutney of your choice.

Enjoy your nutritious and delicious Ragi Dosas as a healthy breakfast or snack! You can also customize the dosas by adding chopped onions, green chilies, or other toppings to the batter before cooking.

Akki Roti (Rice Flour Flatbread)

Ingredients:

- 1 cup rice flour (fine or medium)
- 1 small onion, finely chopped
- 2-3 green chilies, finely chopped (adjust according to spice preference)
- 2 tablespoons chopped fresh coriander leaves
- 1/4 cup grated coconut (optional)
- Salt to taste
- Water, as needed
- Oil or ghee for cooking the rotis

Instructions:

1. In a mixing bowl, combine rice flour, chopped onions, chopped green chilies, chopped coriander leaves, grated coconut (if using), and salt to taste.
2. Gradually add water to the mixture, a little at a time, and knead it into a smooth dough. The dough should be soft and pliable but not too sticky.
3. Divide the dough into equal-sized balls.
4. Take a portion of the dough and flatten it between your palms to form a small disc.
5. Place the flattened dough on a greased sheet of parchment paper or banana leaf.
6. Gently press and spread the dough with your fingertips to form a thin, round roti. If the dough sticks to your fingers, you can wet your fingers with water to prevent sticking.
7. Heat a tawa or skillet over medium heat.
8. Once the tawa is hot, carefully transfer the rolled roti onto it.
9. Cook the roti on one side until small bubbles start to appear on the surface.
10. Flip the roti over using a spatula and cook on the other side until both sides are cooked through and golden brown spots appear.
11. Drizzle a little oil or ghee around the edges of the roti and spread it evenly over the surface.
12. Cook for another minute or two, pressing lightly with the spatula, until the roti is crisp and golden brown.
13. Remove the cooked roti from the tawa and transfer it to a plate.
14. Repeat the process with the remaining dough balls to make more rotis.

15. Serve hot Akki Roti with coconut chutney, pickle, or any curry of your choice.

Enjoy your delicious and gluten-free Akki Roti as a breakfast or snack! You can also customize the recipe by adding grated vegetables or spices to the dough for extra flavor.

Dal Pakwan (Lentil Curry with Fried Bread)

Ingredients:

For Dal (Lentil Curry):

- 1 cup chana dal (split Bengal gram)
- 1/4 teaspoon turmeric powder
- Salt to taste
- 1 tablespoon oil
- 1 teaspoon cumin seeds
- 1 onion, finely chopped
- 2 tomatoes, finely chopped
- 1 green chili, finely chopped (optional)
- 1 teaspoon ginger-garlic paste
- 1/2 teaspoon red chili powder
- 1/2 teaspoon coriander powder
- 1/2 teaspoon garam masala
- 1 tablespoon chopped coriander leaves for garnish
- Lemon wedges for serving (optional)

For Pakwan (Fried Bread):

- 1 cup all-purpose flour (maida)
- 1/4 teaspoon carom seeds (ajwain)
- Salt to taste
- Water, as needed
- Oil for deep frying

Instructions:

1. Prepare the Dal:
    - Rinse the chana dal under cold water and soak it in water for 30 minutes to 1 hour.
    - Drain the soaked dal and transfer it to a pressure cooker.
    - Add turmeric powder, salt, and enough water to cover the dal (about 2 cups).

- Pressure cook the dal for 3-4 whistles or until it is soft and cooked through. Alternatively, you can cook it in a pot until soft.
- Once the pressure releases naturally, open the cooker and mash the dal lightly with a spoon. Set aside.

2. Prepare the Pakwan Dough:
   - In a mixing bowl, combine all-purpose flour, carom seeds, and salt.
   - Gradually add water and knead the mixture into a stiff dough.
   - Cover the dough with a damp cloth and let it rest for 15-20 minutes.

3. Make Pakwan:
   - Divide the rested dough into small lemon-sized balls.
   - Roll out each ball into a thin disc, about 3-4 inches in diameter.
   - Heat oil for deep frying in a kadai or frying pan over medium heat.
   - Once the oil is hot, carefully slide the rolled pakwan into the hot oil.
   - Fry the pakwan until golden brown and crispy on both sides.
   - Remove the fried pakwan from the oil and drain excess oil on paper towels. Set aside.

4. Prepare the Dal Tadka:
   - Heat oil in a pan over medium heat.
   - Add cumin seeds and let them splutter.
   - Add chopped onions and sauté until they turn translucent.
   - Add ginger-garlic paste and chopped green chili (if using). Sauté for a minute until fragrant.
   - Add chopped tomatoes to the pan and cook until they turn soft and mushy.
   - Add red chili powder, coriander powder, and garam masala. Mix well and cook for another minute.
   - Add the cooked and mashed chana dal to the pan. Mix well and simmer for 5-10 minutes until the flavors are well combined.
   - Adjust salt and spices according to taste.

5. Serve:
   - Transfer the prepared dal to a serving bowl.
   - Garnish with chopped coriander leaves.
   - Serve hot Dal Pakwan with lemon wedges on the side for squeezing over the dal.

Enjoy the delicious and flavorful Dal Pakwan for breakfast or as a snack!

Chana Chaat (Chickpea Salad)

Ingredients:

- 2 cups cooked chickpeas (canned or boiled)
- 1 small onion, finely chopped
- 1 small tomato, finely chopped
- 1 small cucumber, finely chopped
- 1 green chili, finely chopped (optional)
- 1/4 cup chopped coriander leaves
- 1/4 cup tamarind chutney
- 1/4 cup green chutney
- 1 tablespoon chaat masala
- 1 teaspoon roasted cumin powder
- 1/2 teaspoon red chili powder (optional)
- Salt to taste
- Lemon wedges for serving
- Sev or crispy fried noodles for garnish (optional)

Instructions:

1. If using canned chickpeas, drain and rinse them under cold water. If using dried chickpeas, soak them overnight, then boil until tender.
2. In a large mixing bowl, combine the cooked chickpeas, chopped onion, tomato, cucumber, green chili (if using), and coriander leaves.
3. Add tamarind chutney and green chutney according to your taste preference. You can adjust the quantity to make the chaat more or less tangy and spicy.
4. Sprinkle chaat masala, roasted cumin powder, red chili powder (if using), and salt over the mixture.
5. Mix everything together until well combined, ensuring that the chickpeas and vegetables are evenly coated with the spices and chutneys.
6. Taste and adjust the seasoning if needed.
7. Transfer the Chana Chaat to serving bowls or plates.
8. Garnish with additional chopped coriander leaves and sev or crispy fried noodles (if using).
9. Serve immediately with lemon wedges on the side for squeezing over the chaat.

Enjoy your delicious and tangy Chana Chaat as a snack or appetizer! You can also customize the chaat by adding other ingredients like boiled potatoes, boiled peanuts, pomegranate seeds, or grated carrots.

Bread Uttapam

Ingredients:

- Bread slices (white or whole wheat)
- 1 cup thick yogurt (curd)
- 1 small onion, finely chopped
- 1 small tomato, finely chopped
- 1/2 small bell pepper (capsicum), finely chopped
- 1 green chili, finely chopped (adjust according to spice preference)
- 1/4 cup chopped coriander leaves
- 1/2 teaspoon cumin seeds
- Salt to taste
- Oil or ghee for cooking the uttapam

Instructions:

1. In a mixing bowl, whisk the thick yogurt until smooth. You can add a little water if the yogurt is too thick.
2. Add chopped onion, tomato, bell pepper, green chili, chopped coriander leaves, cumin seeds, and salt to the yogurt. Mix well to combine all the ingredients.
3. Heat a non-stick skillet or tawa over medium heat.
4. Dip a bread slice into the yogurt mixture, ensuring that both sides are well coated with the mixture.
5. Place the coated bread slice onto the hot skillet and cook for 2-3 minutes on one side until it turns golden brown and crispy.
6. Flip the bread slice over using a spatula and cook for another 2-3 minutes on the other side until cooked through.
7. Repeat the process with the remaining bread slices, coating each slice with the yogurt mixture and cooking them on the skillet until golden brown and crispy.
8. Once all the bread slices are cooked, remove them from the skillet and transfer them to a serving plate.
9. Serve hot Bread Uttapam with coconut chutney, tomato chutney, or any chutney of your choice.

Enjoy your quick and delicious Bread Uttapam as a breakfast or snack! You can also customize the toppings according to your preference by adding grated cheese, sliced vegetables, or paneer.

Egg Biryani

Ingredients:

For Boiling Eggs:

- 4 eggs
- Water, for boiling
- Salt, for boiling

For Rice:

- 1.5 cups basmati rice, soaked for 30 minutes and drained
- Water, for cooking rice
- Salt, to taste

For Biryani Masala:

- 2 onions, thinly sliced
- 2 tomatoes, finely chopped
- 2 green chilies, slit lengthwise
- 1 tablespoon ginger-garlic paste
- 1/2 cup yogurt (curd)
- 1/4 cup chopped mint leaves
- 1/4 cup chopped coriander leaves
- 1 teaspoon red chili powder
- 1/2 teaspoon turmeric powder
- 1 teaspoon biryani masala powder (or garam masala)
- Salt, to taste

For Layering:

- 1/4 cup ghee or oil
- 1/4 cup milk, warmed

- A pinch of saffron strands (optional)
- Fried onions (birista), for garnish
- Chopped coriander leaves, for garnish
- Chopped mint leaves, for garnish

Instructions:

1. Boil the Eggs:
    - Place eggs in a saucepan and cover them with cold water.
    - Add a pinch of salt to the water.
    - Bring the water to a boil over medium-high heat.
    - Once boiling, reduce the heat to low and simmer for 8-10 minutes.
    - Remove the eggs from the hot water and transfer them to a bowl of cold water to cool.
    - Peel the eggs once they are cool enough to handle and set aside.
2. Cook the Rice:
    - In a large pot, bring water to a boil.
    - Add salt to the boiling water.
    - Add soaked and drained basmati rice to the boiling water.
    - Cook the rice until it is 70-80% cooked. It should still have a slight bite to it.
    - Drain the rice and set it aside.
3. Prepare the Biryani Masala:
    - Heat ghee or oil in a large pan or pot over medium heat.
    - Add sliced onions and sauté until golden brown.
    - Add ginger-garlic paste and green chilies. Sauté for a minute until fragrant.
    - Add chopped tomatoes and cook until they turn soft and mushy.
    - Add red chili powder, turmeric powder, biryani masala powder (or garam masala), and salt. Mix well.
    - Add yogurt, chopped mint leaves, and chopped coriander leaves. Cook for 2-3 minutes until the masala is well combined and oil starts to separate from the sides of the pan.
4. Layering the Biryani:
    - In a heavy-bottomed pan or pot, spread a layer of cooked rice evenly at the bottom.
    - Place the boiled eggs on top of the rice in a single layer.
    - Spread the prepared biryani masala evenly over the eggs.
    - Top with the remaining cooked rice, spreading it out evenly.
    - Drizzle warmed milk over the rice.

- If using saffron, soak saffron strands in warm milk for a few minutes and then drizzle over the rice for a rich golden color.
- Cover the pan with a tight-fitting lid.

5. Dum Cooking (Slow Cooking):
    - Place the pan over low heat and let the biryani cook on dum (slow heat) for 20-25 minutes.
    - Alternatively, you can place a tava (griddle) on the stovetop and then place the biryani pot on top of the tava. This helps in even heat distribution and prevents the bottom from burning.
    - Once done, remove the pan from heat and let it rest for 5 minutes before opening the lid.

6. Garnish and Serve:
    - Open the lid of the biryani pot.
    - Garnish with fried onions (birista), chopped coriander leaves, and chopped mint leaves.
    - Serve hot Egg Biryani with raita, salad, or any side dish of your choice.

Enjoy your flavorful and aromatic Egg Biryani as a hearty meal!

Aloo Kachori (Potato Stuffed Savory Pastry)

Ingredients:

For the Dough:

- 2 cups all-purpose flour (maida)
- 1/4 cup ghee or oil
- Salt to taste
- Water, as needed

For the Potato Filling:

- 3-4 medium potatoes, boiled, peeled, and mashed
- 1 onion, finely chopped
- 2 green chilies, finely chopped
- 1 teaspoon ginger-garlic paste
- 1/2 teaspoon cumin seeds
- 1/2 teaspoon turmeric powder
- 1 teaspoon coriander powder
- 1/2 teaspoon garam masala
- 1/2 teaspoon amchur powder (dry mango powder)
- Salt to taste
- Chopped coriander leaves for garnish

For Frying:

- Oil for deep frying

Instructions:

1. Prepare the Dough:
    - In a large mixing bowl, combine all-purpose flour, ghee or oil, and salt.

- Rub the ghee or oil into the flour using your fingertips until the mixture resembles breadcrumbs.
- Gradually add water, a little at a time, and knead the mixture into a smooth and firm dough.
- Cover the dough with a damp cloth and let it rest for 15-20 minutes.

2. Prepare the Potato Filling:
    - Heat oil in a pan over medium heat.
    - Add cumin seeds and let them splutter.
    - Add chopped onions and sauté until they turn translucent.
    - Add ginger-garlic paste and chopped green chilies. Sauté for a minute.
    - Add turmeric powder, coriander powder, garam masala, and amchur powder. Mix well.
    - Add mashed potatoes and salt to taste. Mix until the spices are well combined with the potatoes.
    - Cook the potato mixture for 3-4 minutes, stirring occasionally.
    - Remove from heat and let the filling cool down to room temperature.
    - Once cooled, add chopped coriander leaves and mix well.

3. Shape and Fill the Kachoris:
    - Divide the rested dough into equal-sized balls.
    - Roll out each ball into a small disc, about 3-4 inches in diameter.
    - Place a spoonful of the prepared potato filling onto the center of the disc.
    - Gather the edges of the disc to enclose the filling and seal them properly to form a stuffed ball.
    - Flatten the stuffed ball slightly with your palms.
    - Repeat the process with the remaining dough balls and filling to make more kachoris.

4. Fry the Kachoris:
    - Heat oil for deep frying in a kadai or frying pan over medium heat.
    - Once the oil is hot, carefully slide the stuffed kachoris into the hot oil.
    - Fry the kachoris in batches, flipping occasionally, until they turn golden brown and crisp on all sides.
    - Remove the fried kachoris from the oil using a slotted spoon and drain excess oil on paper towels.

5. Serve:
    - Serve hot Aloo Kachoris with mint chutney, tamarind chutney, or yogurt.

Enjoy your crispy and delicious Aloo Kachoris as a snack or appetizer!

Rava Idli (Semolina Steamed Cakes)

Ingredients:

- 1 cup fine semolina (rava or sooji)
- 1 cup plain yogurt (curd)
- 1/2 cup water, or as needed
- 1/2 teaspoon baking soda
- Salt to taste
- 1 tablespoon oil or ghee
- 1 teaspoon mustard seeds
- 1 teaspoon urad dal (split black gram lentils)
- 1 teaspoon chana dal (split Bengal gram lentils)
- 1/2 teaspoon finely chopped ginger
- 1 green chili, finely chopped (optional)
- A few curry leaves, torn into pieces
- 1 tablespoon chopped coriander leaves (optional)
- Cashews or grated coconut for garnish (optional)

Instructions:

1. In a mixing bowl, combine semolina, plain yogurt, and salt. Mix well to form a smooth batter. Add water gradually to adjust the consistency. The batter should be thick yet pourable. Let it rest for 10-15 minutes.
2. Heat oil or ghee in a small pan over medium heat. Add mustard seeds and let them splutter. Add urad dal, chana dal, chopped ginger, chopped green chili (if using), and torn curry leaves. Sauté until the dals turn golden brown.
3. Add the tempering to the semolina batter and mix well. Adjust the consistency of the batter if needed by adding a little more water.
4. Grease the idli molds with oil or ghee. If using an electric idli steamer, preheat it.
5. Just before steaming, add baking soda to the batter and mix gently. The batter will become frothy.
6. Pour the batter into the greased idli molds, filling them about 3/4 full. Garnish with chopped coriander leaves, cashews, or grated coconut if desired.
7. Steam the idlis in an idli steamer or pressure cooker without the whistle for about 10-12 minutes, or until a toothpick inserted into the center comes out clean.

8. Once done, remove the idli molds from the steamer and let them cool for a few minutes.
9. Carefully remove the idlis from the molds using a spoon or butter knife.
10. Serve hot Rava Idlis with coconut chutney, tomato chutney, or sambar.

Enjoy your soft and fluffy Rava Idlis for a delicious and nutritious breakfast!

Sabudana Vada (Tapioca Pearl Fritters)

Ingredients:

- 1 cup sabudana (tapioca pearls)
- 2 medium potatoes, boiled and mashed
- 1/2 cup roasted peanuts, coarsely ground
- 2 green chilies, finely chopped
- 1 teaspoon cumin seeds
- 1 teaspoon grated ginger
- 1 tablespoon chopped coriander leaves
- 1 tablespoon lemon juice
- Salt to taste
- Oil for frying

Instructions:

1. Rinse the sabudana under cold water until the water runs clear. Soak the sabudana in enough water to cover them completely for at least 4-5 hours or overnight. After soaking, the sabudana should be soft and plump.
2. Drain the soaked sabudana using a colander to remove excess water. Transfer the drained sabudana to a large mixing bowl.
3. Add boiled and mashed potatoes, coarsely ground roasted peanuts, chopped green chilies, cumin seeds, grated ginger, chopped coriander leaves, lemon juice, and salt to taste to the bowl with the drained sabudana.
4. Mix all the ingredients well to form a uniform mixture. The mixture should be soft and slightly sticky.
5. Heat oil in a deep frying pan or kadai over medium heat.
6. While the oil is heating, shape the sabudana mixture into small patties or vadas. Take a small portion of the mixture, roll it into a ball, and then flatten it slightly to form a patty shape. Repeat with the remaining mixture.
7. Once the oil is hot, carefully slide the shaped sabudana vadas into the hot oil, a few at a time.
8. Fry the sabudana vadas on medium heat until they turn golden brown and crispy on all sides. Make sure to flip them occasionally for even cooking.
9. Once done, remove the fried sabudana vadas using a slotted spoon and drain excess oil on paper towels.

10. Serve hot Sabudana Vadas with green chutney, sweetened yogurt, or coconut chutney.

Enjoy your crispy and delicious Sabudana Vadas as a snack or appetizer!

Chutney Sandwich

Ingredients:

- Bread slices (white or whole wheat)
- Green chutney (mint-coriander chutney or any chutney of your choice)
- Butter or margarine (optional)
- Sliced vegetables (such as cucumber, tomato, onion, capsicum)
- Salt and pepper to taste (optional)

Instructions:

1. Prepare the Green Chutney:
    - If you don't have ready-made green chutney, you can make it at home by blending together fresh mint leaves, coriander leaves, green chilies, ginger, garlic, lemon juice, salt, and a little water to form a smooth paste. Adjust the ingredients according to your taste preference.
2. Assemble the Sandwich:
    - Take two slices of bread and spread a generous amount of green chutney on one slice. You can also butter the other slice if you like.
    - Place the sliced vegetables (cucumber, tomato, onion, capsicum) on top of the chutney-covered bread slice.
    - Sprinkle salt and pepper to taste over the vegetables, if desired.
    - Close the sandwich with the other bread slice, pressing down gently to seal the filling inside.
3. Cut and Serve:
    - Using a sharp knife, cut the sandwich diagonally into two triangles or into smaller bite-sized pieces.
    - Serve the Chutney Sandwich immediately as a snack or pack it for a lunchbox.

Enjoy your refreshing and flavorful Chutney Sandwich with your favorite chutney and vegetable fillings! You can also customize the sandwich by adding cheese slices, boiled eggs, or any other fillings of your choice.

Chole Kulcha (Chickpea Curry with Flatbread)

Ingredients:

For Chole (Chickpea Curry):

- 1 cup dried chickpeas (chole), soaked overnight or for at least 6-8 hours
- 2 tablespoons oil or ghee
- 1 large onion, finely chopped
- 2 tomatoes, finely chopped
- 1-2 green chilies, slit lengthwise
- 1 tablespoon ginger-garlic paste
- 1 teaspoon cumin seeds
- 1 teaspoon coriander powder
- 1/2 teaspoon turmeric powder
- 1 teaspoon red chili powder (adjust to taste)
- 1 teaspoon garam masala
- 1 teaspoon dried mango powder (amchur)
- Salt to taste
- Water, as needed
- Chopped coriander leaves for garnish

For Kulcha (Flatbread):

- 2 cups all-purpose flour (maida)
- 1/2 cup yogurt (curd)
- 1 teaspoon baking powder
- 1/2 teaspoon baking soda
- 1/2 teaspoon sugar
- Salt to taste
- Water, as needed
- Butter or ghee for brushing

Instructions:

1. Prepare Chole (Chickpea Curry):
   - Rinse the soaked chickpeas under cold water and drain.
   - Heat oil or ghee in a pressure cooker or large pot over medium heat.
   - Add cumin seeds and let them splutter.
   - Add chopped onions and sauté until they turn translucent.
   - Add ginger-garlic paste and slit green chilies. Sauté for a minute until fragrant.
   - Add chopped tomatoes and cook until they turn soft and mushy.
   - Add coriander powder, turmeric powder, red chili powder, and salt. Mix well.
   - Add soaked chickpeas to the pot along with water. The water level should be about 1-2 inches above the chickpeas.
   - Close the pressure cooker lid and cook for 5-6 whistles or until the chickpeas are soft and cooked through. If using a pot, cover and cook until chickpeas are tender, adding more water if needed.
   - Once done, open the pressure cooker carefully and check the consistency of the curry. If it's too thin, simmer for a few more minutes until it thickens slightly.
   - Add garam masala and dried mango powder (amchur). Mix well.
   - Garnish with chopped coriander leaves and set aside.
2. Prepare Kulcha (Flatbread):
   - In a large mixing bowl, combine all-purpose flour, yogurt, baking powder, baking soda, sugar, and salt.
   - Mix well and knead into a soft dough, adding water as needed. The dough should be smooth and elastic.
   - Cover the dough with a damp cloth and let it rest for 2 hours.
3. Shape and Cook Kulcha:
   - After resting, divide the dough into equal-sized balls.
   - Roll out each ball into a small disc or oval shape, about 1/4 inch thick.
   - Heat a tawa or skillet over medium heat.
   - Place the rolled kulcha on the hot tawa and cook for 1-2 minutes on one side until bubbles start to form.
   - Flip the kulcha over and cook on the other side until golden brown spots appear.
   - Brush with butter or ghee while cooking.
   - Remove the cooked kulcha from the tawa and set aside. Repeat with the remaining dough balls.
4. Serve Chole Kulcha:
   - Serve hot Chole with freshly cooked Kulcha.

- Garnish with additional chopped coriander leaves if desired.
- Enjoy your delicious Chole Kulcha!

This flavorful and satisfying dish is perfect for breakfast, brunch, or lunch, and it's sure to be a hit with family and friends!

Egg Curry Puff

Ingredients:

For the Pastry:

- 2 cups all-purpose flour
- 1/2 teaspoon salt
- 1/2 cup unsalted butter, cold and cubed
- 1/2 cup cold water

For the Egg Curry Filling:

- 4 hard-boiled eggs, chopped
- 1 onion, finely chopped
- 2 cloves garlic, minced
- 1 teaspoon grated ginger
- 1 tomato, finely chopped
- 1 green chili, finely chopped (optional)
- 1 teaspoon curry powder
- 1/2 teaspoon turmeric powder
- 1/2 teaspoon garam masala
- Salt to taste
- 2 tablespoons chopped coriander leaves
- Oil for cooking

Instructions:

1. Prepare the Pastry:
    - In a large mixing bowl, combine the all-purpose flour and salt.
    - Add the cold cubed butter to the flour mixture.
    - Using your fingertips, rub the butter into the flour until the mixture resembles breadcrumbs.
    - Gradually add the cold water, a little at a time, and mix until a dough forms. Be careful not to overwork the dough.

- Wrap the dough in plastic wrap and refrigerate for at least 30 minutes.
2. Prepare the Egg Curry Filling:
    - Heat oil in a pan over medium heat.
    - Add the chopped onion and sauté until translucent.
    - Add the minced garlic and grated ginger. Sauté for another minute until fragrant.
    - Add the chopped tomato and green chili (if using). Cook until the tomato softens.
    - Stir in the curry powder, turmeric powder, and garam masala. Cook for a few seconds until the spices are fragrant.
    - Add the chopped hard-boiled eggs to the pan and mix well with the spice mixture.
    - Season with salt to taste and cook for another 2-3 minutes.
    - Stir in the chopped coriander leaves. Remove from heat and let the filling cool slightly.
3. Assemble the Egg Curry Puffs:
    - Preheat the oven to 200°C (400°F) and line a baking sheet with parchment paper.
    - Remove the chilled dough from the refrigerator and roll it out on a floured surface to about 1/4 inch thickness.
    - Use a round cookie cutter or a glass to cut out circles from the dough.
    - Place a spoonful of the cooled egg curry filling in the center of each dough circle.
    - Fold the dough over the filling to form a half-moon shape and seal the edges by pressing with a fork.
    - Place the assembled puffs onto the prepared baking sheet.
    - Optional: Brush the tops of the puffs with beaten egg for a shiny finish.
4. Bake the Egg Curry Puffs:
    - Bake in the preheated oven for 20-25 minutes or until the puffs are golden brown and crispy.
    - Remove from the oven and let cool slightly before serving.
5. Serve:
    - Enjoy the Egg Curry Puffs warm as a delicious snack or appetizer.

These Egg Curry Puffs are perfect for picnics, parties, or as a tasty snack any time of the day!

Aloo Methi Paratha (Potato Fenugreek Stuffed Bread)

Ingredients:

For the Dough:

- 2 cups whole wheat flour (atta)
- Water, as needed
- Salt, to taste
- Oil or ghee, for cooking

For the Filling:

- 2 medium-sized potatoes, boiled and mashed
- 1 cup fresh fenugreek leaves (methi), finely chopped
- 1 small onion, finely chopped
- 2 green chilies, finely chopped (adjust to taste)
- 1 teaspoon grated ginger
- 1/2 teaspoon cumin seeds
- 1/2 teaspoon turmeric powder
- 1 teaspoon coriander powder
- 1/2 teaspoon garam masala
- Salt, to taste
- Fresh coriander leaves, chopped (optional)

Instructions:

1. Prepare the Dough:
    - In a large mixing bowl, combine whole wheat flour and salt.
    - Gradually add water and knead to form a soft and smooth dough. The dough should be pliable and not too stiff or too sticky.
    - Cover the dough with a damp cloth and let it rest for 15-20 minutes.
2. Prepare the Filling:
    - Heat oil in a pan over medium heat.
    - Add cumin seeds and let them splutter.

- Add chopped onions and sauté until translucent.
- Add grated ginger and chopped green chilies. Sauté for a minute.
- Add chopped fenugreek leaves (methi) and cook until they wilt and become soft.
- Add turmeric powder, coriander powder, garam masala, and salt. Mix well.
- Add mashed potatoes to the pan and mix until all the ingredients are well combined.
- Cook the filling for another 2-3 minutes, stirring occasionally.
- Optional: Add chopped fresh coriander leaves for added flavor. Remove the filling from heat and let it cool slightly.

3. Assemble and Cook the Parathas:
   - Divide the rested dough into equal-sized balls.
   - Take a dough ball and roll it out into a small circle on a floured surface.
   - Place a spoonful of the prepared potato-fenugreek filling in the center of the circle.
   - Gather the edges of the dough to enclose the filling and pinch to seal the edges.
   - Flatten the stuffed dough ball gently with your palms.
   - Roll out the stuffed dough ball into a paratha, using a rolling pin. Be gentle to ensure the filling doesn't come out.
   - Heat a tawa or skillet over medium heat.
   - Place the rolled paratha onto the hot tawa and cook for a minute or two on one side until small bubbles start to form.
   - Flip the paratha over and cook on the other side, applying a little oil or ghee on both sides, until golden brown spots appear.
   - Repeat the process with the remaining dough balls and filling to make more parathas.

4. Serve:
   - Serve the hot Aloo Methi Parathas with yogurt, pickle, or any chutney of your choice.
   - Enjoy the delicious and flavorful parathas as a breakfast or main course dish!

These Aloo Methi Parathas are not only tasty but also packed with the goodness of fenugreek leaves and potatoes, making them a wholesome meal option.

Khaman Dhokla (Gram Flour Steamed Cake)

Ingredients:

For the Batter:

- 1 cup gram flour (besan)
- 1/4 cup semolina (sooji)
- 1/4 cup yogurt (curd)
- 1 tablespoon oil
- 1 teaspoon ginger-green chili paste
- 1/2 teaspoon turmeric powder
- 1 teaspoon sugar
- Salt to taste
- 1 cup water
- 1 teaspoon eno fruit salt or baking soda
- 1 tablespoon lemon juice

For Tempering:

- 2 tablespoons oil
- 1 teaspoon mustard seeds
- 1 teaspoon sesame seeds (optional)
- 2-3 green chilies, slit lengthwise
- A few curry leaves
- 2 tablespoons chopped coriander leaves
- 2 tablespoons grated coconut (optional)
- 2 tablespoons water
- 1 tablespoon sugar
- 2 tablespoons lemon juice
- Salt to taste

Instructions:

1. Prepare the Batter:

- In a large mixing bowl, combine gram flour, semolina, yogurt, oil, ginger-green chili paste, turmeric powder, sugar, and salt.
- Gradually add water to the mixture, stirring continuously, to make a smooth batter without any lumps.
- Let the batter rest for 15-20 minutes to allow the semolina to absorb moisture.

2. Prepare the Steamer:
   - Meanwhile, fill a steamer or a large pot with water and bring it to a boil. Place a steaming rack inside the steamer.
3. Steam the Dhokla:
   - Grease a round cake tin or thali with oil and set it aside.
   - Just before steaming, add eno fruit salt or baking soda to the batter and mix well. The batter will become frothy.
   - Immediately pour the batter into the greased cake tin or thali and spread it evenly.
4. Steam the batter in the preheated steamer for 15-20 minutes or until a toothpick inserted into the center comes out clean.
5. Prepare the Tempering:
   - Heat oil in a small pan over medium heat for tempering.
   - Add mustard seeds and let them splutter.
   - Add sesame seeds (if using), slit green chilies, and curry leaves. Sauté for a few seconds.
   - Add water, sugar, lemon juice, and salt to the tempering mixture. Stir well and let it simmer for a minute.
   - Remove from heat and set aside.
6. Once the Dhokla is steamed, remove it from the steamer and let it cool for a few minutes.
7. Cut the Dhokla into squares or diamond shapes using a knife.
8. Pour the prepared tempering over the cut Dhokla pieces, ensuring that the tempering mixture seeps into the slits.
9. Garnish the Dhokla with chopped coriander leaves and grated coconut (if using).
10. Serve the Khaman Dhokla warm or at room temperature with green chutney or tamarind chutney.

Enjoy the soft, fluffy, and tangy Khaman Dhokla as a delightful snack or breakfast item!

Rajma Chawal (Kidney Bean Curry with Rice)

Ingredients:

For Rajma (Kidney Bean Curry):

- 1 cup dried kidney beans (rajma), soaked overnight or for at least 8 hours
- 2 tablespoons oil or ghee
- 1 teaspoon cumin seeds
- 1 large onion, finely chopped
- 2 tomatoes, finely chopped
- 1 tablespoon ginger-garlic paste
- 2 green chilies, slit lengthwise
- 1 teaspoon Kashmiri red chili powder (or regular chili powder)
- 1 teaspoon coriander powder
- 1/2 teaspoon turmeric powder
- 1 teaspoon garam masala
- Salt to taste
- Water, as needed
- Chopped coriander leaves for garnish

For Chawal (Steamed Rice):

- 1 cup basmati rice
- Water, as needed
- Salt, to taste

Instructions:

1. Prepare Rajma (Kidney Bean Curry):
    - Rinse the soaked kidney beans under cold water and drain.
    - In a pressure cooker, heat oil or ghee over medium heat.
    - Add cumin seeds and let them splutter.
    - Add chopped onions and sauté until golden brown.

- Add ginger-garlic paste and slit green chilies. Sauté for a minute until fragrant.
- Add chopped tomatoes and cook until they turn soft and mushy.
- Add Kashmiri red chili powder, coriander powder, turmeric powder, garam masala, and salt. Mix well.
- Add the soaked kidney beans to the pressure cooker along with water. The water level should be about 1-2 inches above the beans.
- Close the pressure cooker lid and cook for 6-7 whistles or until the beans are soft and cooked through. If using a pot, cover and cook until beans are tender, adding more water if needed.
- Once done, open the pressure cooker carefully and check the consistency of the curry. If it's too thin, simmer for a few more minutes until it thickens slightly.
- Garnish with chopped coriander leaves and set aside.

2. Prepare Chawal (Steamed Rice):
   - Rinse the basmati rice under cold water until the water runs clear.
   - In a large pot, bring water to a boil over medium-high heat.
   - Add salt to the boiling water.
   - Add the rinsed basmati rice to the boiling water and cook until the rice is tender but still has a slight bite to it.
   - Once done, drain the cooked rice using a colander and let any excess water drain off.

3. Serve:
   - Serve the hot Rajma Curry with steamed rice (Chawal).
   - Garnish with additional chopped coriander leaves if desired.
   - Enjoy your comforting and delicious Rajma Chawal!

Rajma Chawal is often served with sliced onions, lemon wedges, and a side of pickle or yogurt for a complete meal experience.

Anda Pav (Egg Sandwich)

Ingredients:

For the Scrambled Eggs:

- 4 eggs
- 1 small onion, finely chopped
- 1 small tomato, finely chopped
- 1 green chili, finely chopped (optional)
- 1/2 teaspoon turmeric powder
- 1/2 teaspoon red chili powder
- 1/2 teaspoon garam masala
- Salt to taste
- 2 tablespoons oil or butter
- Chopped coriander leaves for garnish

For Serving:

- Pav (soft bread rolls)
- Butter for toasting the pav
- Tomato ketchup or green chutney (optional)

Instructions:

1. Prepare the Scrambled Eggs:
    - In a bowl, crack the eggs and whisk them until well beaten.
    - Heat oil or butter in a pan over medium heat.
    - Add chopped onions and sauté until they turn translucent.
    - Add chopped tomatoes and green chilies (if using). Cook until the tomatoes soften.
    - Lower the heat and add turmeric powder, red chili powder, garam masala, and salt. Mix well.
    - Pour the beaten eggs into the pan and let them cook for a few seconds.

- Using a spatula, scramble the eggs gently until they are cooked through and slightly moist.
- Remove the scrambled eggs from heat and garnish with chopped coriander leaves. Set aside.

2. Prepare the Pav:
    - Slice the pav horizontally into halves, keeping them attached on one side.
    - Heat a griddle or skillet over medium heat.
    - Spread butter on the cut sides of the pav.
    - Toast the buttered pav on the griddle until they turn golden brown and crisp on the edges. Remove from heat.
3. Assemble Anda Pav:
    - Place a generous portion of the prepared scrambled eggs between the toasted pav halves.
    - Optionally, add a dollop of tomato ketchup or green chutney on top of the scrambled eggs for extra flavor.
    - Press the pav gently to close the sandwich.
4. Serve:
    - Serve the Anda Pav hot as a delicious and satisfying breakfast, brunch, or snack.
    - You can wrap the Anda Pav in butter paper or serve it on a plate with additional ketchup or chutney on the side.

Enjoy your homemade Anda Pav with its delightful combination of fluffy scrambled eggs and buttery pav!